For Starters

For Starters

INGEBORG PERTWEE

World's Work Ltd

Photography by John Barrett
Line Drawings by John Spencer

Text copyright © 1984 by Ingeborg Pertwee
Published by
World's Work Ltd
The Windmill Press, Kingswood,
Tadworth, Surrey

ISBN 0 437 12723 0

Typeset by Words & Pictures Ltd, London
Printed and bound in Great Britain by
Biddles Ltd. Guildford and Kings Lynn

Contents

ARTICHOKE

ASPARAGUS

AUBERGINE

SALAD DRESSINGS AND SAUCES

Illustrations

The following recipes are illustrated in colour.

Between pages 48 and 49

Beetroot Sorbet, Celery and Apple Sorbet
Minted Grape and Melon Cocktail
Cucumber and Yoghurt Mousse
Avocados Stuffed with Crab
Mozarella and Tomato Salad

Between pages 112 and 113

Brown Bean Soup, Elegant Cheese Soup, Quick Iced
    Asparagus Soup
Mussels in Dilled Cucumber Sauce
Marinated Mushrooms, Marinated Bean Salad
Tuna Salad Niçoise
Apples Stuffed with Crabmeat, Lemons Stuffed
    with Sardine Mousse

Between pages 208 and 209

Hasty Pâté, Mushroom and Carrot Pâté, Scampi Pâté
Turkey and Strawberry Cocktail
Smoked Chicken and Blue Cheese Salad
Bel's Quick Tomato Starter, Tomato Gervais, Tomato Rose,
    Accordion Tomato
Snails in Herb Butter

Introduction

The first course, also referred to as 'starter', 'appetizer', or 'hors d'oeuvre', is the overture to a meal. Not only does it indicate the quality of the repast to come, it also determines the balance of the whole meal.

Never too filling, the starter should merely whet the appetite and never suffocate it. It should never prevail over the following courses in quantity or texture, so that a refreshing, light starter should always precede a heavy, rich dish.

Seasons also play an important part. Chilled soups, iced fruit or shellfish cocktails are essential summer starters, whilst aromatic pâtés, marinated fish or hot soups fare better in cooler seasons. There are hot and cold starters which can be prepared ahead of time. There are starters that can be produced from left-overs and others requiring more exotic ingredients. All of them have something in common: the purpose of stimulating the appetite.

This was realized as early as the third century BC when Athens had developed the original hors d'oeuvre trolley. In Baghdad, during the tenth century BC, the banquets given at the courts of the Caliphs were not only renowned for their extravagance, but also for their poetry and gastronomic erudition of conversation. A guest of Caliph Mustakfi composed a poem describing a tray of hors d'oeuvre. The Romans started their meals with salads, cooked vegetables, fungi, light egg or fish dishes.

Later, during the seventeenth century in England, starters consisted of a salad of herbs and eggs, often further enhanced by the addition of cold roast capon, anchovies, or other meat or fish delicacies. But these starters were only offered to special guests and were not part of the every-day meal. In eighteenth-century France hors d'oeuvre were sometimes called *'entrées volantes'* or *'assiettes volantes'* (flying entrées or flying dishes). It is not quite clear though if they were light dishes which 'flew' down the throat, or if they were passed only once by the servants and not put on the table, as was the custom.

In spite of its long culinary history, the starter is often neglected; little imagination is given to its preparation, yet there are hundreds of variations which can make the first course an enticing, appetizing dish.

I have always regarded the starter as the most important part of any meal and I hope that the following collection of my favourite recipes will help to revive the starter's good name.

Ingeborg Pertwee

13

Tables of Conversion

Quantities in these recipes are given in both imperial and metric measures. Use either one or the other measure, but never both in the same recipe as metric measures have been rounded off to the nearest 25 grammes for convenience.

Below is a table of recommended equivalents.

Ounces/fluid ounces	Approx g and ml to nearest whole figure	Recommended conversion to nearest unit of 25 g
1	28	25
2	57	50
3	85	75
4	113	100
5 (¼ pint)	142	150
6	170	175
7	198	200
8 (½ lb.)	226	225
9	255	250
10 (½ pint)	283	275
11	311	300
12	340	350
13	368	375
14	396	400
15 (¾ pint)	428	425
16 (1 lb.)	456	450
17	484	475
18	512	500
19	541	550
20 (1 pint)	569	575

Oven temperatures
Below are given recommended Celsius (Centigrade) equivalents.

Description	Fahrenheit	Celsius	Gas Mark
Very cool	225	110	¼
	250	130	½
Cool	275	140	1
	300	150	2
Moderate	325	170	3
	350	180	4
Moderately hot	375	190	5
	400	200	6
Hot	425	220	7
	450	230	8
Very hot	475	240	9

Artichoke

A close friend of the thistle, the artichoke goes back as far as 200AD, to the days of the ancient Romans who already had begun to cultivate it. Catherine de Medici loved artichokes and carried them to France when she became the wife of Henry II. Since then, *fonds d'artichauts* (artichoke hearts) have achieved their mark among gourmets.

Europe and Australia produce a conical shaped artichoke, known as 'Tuscany violet' and 'Paris green' while the globe, or green artichoke, is produced in California.

Do not confuse them with the 'Jerusalem artichoke', which is of entirely different origin.

Tips

■ When selecting artichokes, choose those with tight heads and large fleshy leaves.
■ Avoid those whose leaves have opened indicating that they are over-mature.
■ The *fond d'artichaut* is the delicate heart, which can be bought tinned or frozen and used in salads, seafood starters, dressed with mayonnaise or French dressing.

To Trim Artichokes into Artichoke Hearts

1. Cut off and discard the stems.
2. Bend back the outer leaves until they snap off close to the base. Remove several more layers of leaves in the same way until the pale inner leaves are reached.
3-4. Trim the base and sides with a stainless steel knife.
5. Cut off the top ½ inch/1 cm of the artichoke heart. Half the artichoke heart lengthwise and rub the surface with half a lemon to prevent discolouring. Drop each heart as it is trimmed, into a bowl of cold, acidulated water.

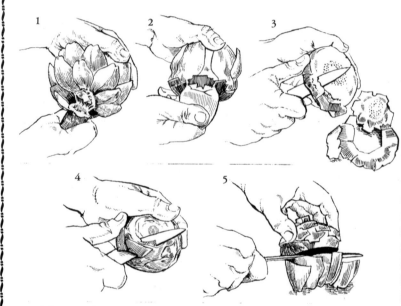

To Cook Fresh Artichoke Hearts

Boil the artichoke hearts in salted water, acidulated with the juice of half a lemon, for 12-15 minutes, or until the hearts are tender.

Drain them in a colander, refresh under running cold water and pat dry.

ARTICHOKE VINAIGRETTE

2 small or 1 large artichoke per person
French dressing, see page 265
salt

Wash the artichokes, cut off the stalks and the outer row of leaves. With sharp kitchen scissors trim the tops of all the other leaves.
In a large saucepan bring salted water to boil. Plunge the artichokes into the boiling water and cook, uncovered, for about 30 minutes, or until the inside leaves pull out easily. Drain the artichokes upside-down to remove the water. Serve on individual plates with the French dressing served separately.

To eat them:
The leaves are torn off one by one, the base of each leaf being dipped into the dressing and the soft end pulled off by the teeth. The small inner leaves and the bristly centre are discarded, leaving the best part, the heart, which is eaten with knife and fork.

ARTICHOKES WITH MOCK CAVIAR

4 large or 8 small artichokes, fresh, frozen or tinned
1 small jar red lump fish (mock caviar)
1 (5 fl oz/142 ml) carton sour cream
freshly ground black pepper
lemon wedges

If fresh, prepare the artichoke hearts as directed on page 18.
Mix the lump fish with the sour cream.
Add freshly ground black pepper.
Spread the mixture over the hearts.
Serve on chilled individual plates. Garnish with lemon wedges.
Serves 4

ARTICHOKE WITH LEMON MAYONNAISE

4 large artichokes
salt
2 teaspoons olive oil
rind and juice of 1 lemon
4-6 tablespoons mayonnaise, see page 266
fresh parsley, chopped
freshly ground black pepper

Cut the stems from the artichokes and trim the tops of the leaves. Put the artichokes into boiling salted water with the olive oil.
Cook, uncovered, for 30 minutes, or until the leaves pull out easily.
Drain the artichokes upside-down, squeezing gently to remove the water.
Cool slightly, then remove the centre.
Grate the lemon rind, squeeze out the juice and blend with the mayonnaise. Season with black pepper.
Spoon the mayonnaise into the centre of the artichokes.
Sprinkle with parsley. Serve the artichokes cold.
Serves 4

ARTICHOKE HEARTS WITH CRABMEAT

4 large or 8 small artichokes, fresh, frozen or tinned
1 tin crabmeat, drained
mayonnaise, see page 266
cayenne pepper
crisp lettuce leaves

If fresh prepare the artichoke hearts as directed on page 18.
Dress the crabmeat with the mayonnaise.
Pile the mixture on each heart. Sprinkle with cayenne pepper.
Serve on chilled, individual plates lined with lettuce leaves.
Serves 4

ARTICHOKE HEARTS IN JELLY

*This recipe is both simple and quick and can be prepared
well in advance.*

1 tin artichoke hearts, drained
1 tin consommé
3 tablespoons small peas, cooked
1 tablespoon white wine vinegar
1 tablespoon fresh tarragon, chopped
(if not available mint may be used)

Dice the artichoke hearts.
Dissolve the consommé over gentle heat. Add the peas,
artichokes, vinegar and tarragon.
Pour the mixture into individual small dishes and leave to
cool.
Chill for several hours in the refrigerator.
Serves 4

ARTICHOKE HEARTS WITH MUSHROOMS

4 large or 8 small artichoke hearts, fresh, frozen or tinned
1½ oz/40 g butter
8 oz/225 g mushrooms
¼ pint/150 ml thick béchamel sauce, see page 270
salt and freshly ground black pepper
1 oz/25 g Gruyère cheese, grated

If fresh, prepare the artichokes as directed on page 18.
Sauté them gently in half of the butter. Remove them to a
warm ovenproof serving dish.
Wash, trim and slice the mushrooms. Sauté them in the
remaining butter.
Make the béchamel sauce. Blend in the mushrooms. Season
with salt and pepper.
Fill the hearts with the mixture. Sprinkle with grated cheese.
Brown under the grill until golden.
Serves 4

ARTICHOKE HEARTS WITH EGGS AND CREAM

4 large or 8 small artichoke hearts, fresh, frozen or tinned
1 tablespoon dried *fines herbes*
½ pint/300 ml double cream
juice of half a lemon
4 eggs, soft-boiled and shelled
salt and freshly ground black pepper

If fresh, prepare the artichokes as directed on page 18.
In a bowl combine the *fines herbes*, 2½ tablespoons of the cream and the lemon juice. Mix well and spoon into the artichoke hearts. Place a soft-boiled egg on each heart.
Whip the remaining cream, season with salt and pepper, and heap this on top of the eggs.
Chill for several hours.
Serves 4

ARTICHOKE HEARTS WITH STILTON

12 small artichoke hearts, fresh, frozen or tinned
4 tablespoons olive oil
1 small onion, finely chopped
1 clove of garlic, crushed
2 tablespoons lemon juice
2 oz/50 g Stilton, or any other similar blue cheese,
crumbled
1 tablespoon fresh parsley, finely chopped

In a heavy saucepan heat the oil. Add the onion and garlic and cook for 5 minutes, stirring, or until the onion is soft. Add the artichoke hearts and cook over moderate heat, stirring, until thoroughly heated through. Add the lemon juice. Remove the pan from the heat. Add the Stilton and toss until the cheese is melted.
Transfer to a serving dish. Sprinkle with parsley.
Serve hot.
Serves 4-6

ARTICHOKES WITH SPINACH

4 large or 8 small artichokes, fresh, frozen or tinned
juice of 1 lemon (only if hearts are fresh)
1 lb/450 g spinach
4 tablespoons double cream
salt and freshly ground black pepper
1 oz/25 g Cheddar cheese, grated
1 oz/25 g Parmesan cheese, grated

If fresh, prepare the artichokes as directed on page 16.
Wash the spinach thoroughly, discarding the stalks.
Cook the spinach in a saucepan with very little water for 10 minutes. Drain off excess water.
Blend the spinach together with the cream in an electric blender or mixer. Season with pepper and very little salt.
Arrange the well drained artichoke hearts in a baking dish large enough to hold them in one layer.
Spoon the spinach and cream mixture into the centre of each heart.
Mix the Cheddar with the Parmesan cheese. Sprinkle it over the spinach.
Bake at 350°F/180°C/Gas Mark 4 for 10 minutes in the oven, or until golden brown.
Serve immediately.
Serves 4

ARTICHOKE HEARTS WITH POACHED EGGS AND MAYONNAISE

6 large or 12 small artichoke hearts,
fresh, frozen or tinned
2 tablespoons cider- or white wine vinegar
6 large eggs
8 tablespoons mayonnaise, see page 266
salt and freshly ground black pepper
watercress for garnish

If fresh prepare the artichoke hearts as directed on page 18.
Fill a shallow, wide saucepan full of water and add the vinegar. Bring to boil over high heat, then reduce heat so that the liquid barely simmers.
Break the eggs, one at a time, into a saucer and slide them into the liquid. As each egg drops in, push the egg white gently towards the yolk.
Simmer the eggs for 3 minutes, then transfer them with a slotted spoon to a bowl of cold water.
Season the artichoke hearts with salt and pepper. Arrange them on individual serving plates.
Spread 1 tablespoon mayonnaise on each heart. With the slotted spoon drain the eggs carefully, pat dry and trim edges.
Arrange 1 egg on each artichoke heart. Spoon a little mayonnaise on top.
Garnish with watercress sprigs. Serve cold.
Serves 6

ROMAN ARTICHOKES

6 large or 12 small artichokes
lemon slices
2 oz/50 g breadcrumbs
2 cloves of garlic, crushed
fresh mint, chopped
salt and black pepper
3 tablespoons olive oil
¼ pint/150 ml water

Remove the outer leaves from the artichokes. Trim the tops of the remaining leaves and the hard part from the inside leaves. Clean the artichoke leaves and the heart.

Trim the stems to a length of 2 inches. Rub the ends with slices of lemon to prevent them from becoming black.

Using your fingers, open the leaves wide and fill the empty centre with a mixture of crushed garlic, breadcrumbs, chopped mint and salt and pepper. Moisten the mixture with a little oil. Push the leaves tightly back into place so that the stuffing remains intact.

Arrange the artichokes, with the stems facing upwards, in an ovenproof dish large enough to hold them in one layer.

Pour water into the dish, cover the artichokes with a sheet of greaseproof paper brushed with oil, then cover the dish tightly. Cook the artichokes in a hot oven (425°F/220°C/Gas Mark 7) for about 1 hour.

Serve hot.

Serves 6

QUICK SALAD OF ARTICHOKE HEARTS

1 tin artichoke hearts, drained
1 medium onion
1 (4 oz/100 g) tin red kidney beans, drained
French dressing, see page 265
3 rashers streaky bacon

Slice the artichoke hearts into quarters.

Slice the onion into rings and mix with the artichokes.

Remove the rinds from the bacon and chop the rashers.

Fry the rinds until the fat runs, then fry the bacon pieces and rinds together until very crisp.

Place them on an absorbent kitchen paper towel to drain.

Cool and crumble the bacon.

Stir the beans and French dressing into the artichokes and onion and sprinkle the crumbled bacon over the top.

Serve very cold.

Serves 4

Asparagus

The name 'asparagus' is derived from the Greek word for sprout, 'asparagos'. But it was the Romans who cultivated this member of the lily family, which until then had been known only in its wild state.

There are over a hundred different species, but we only need to be concerned with two kinds: white and green asparagus. There has always reigned fierce controversy over the question of superiority. French experts insist that white asparagus, which is brought to maturity underground and so kept from becoming green, is far more delicate and tender. Defenders of green asparagus argue that white asparagus is tasteless and cannot be compared to the variety which gets its flavour from the sunlight.

Asparagus arrived in England in the early seventeenth century, 'I will have asparagus every meale all the yeare long', said William Broome (1689-1745).

Asparagus became so popular that in 1815 asparagus tongs were invented.

Asparagus contains calcium, iron, potassium and vitamins C, B and A.
4 oz/100 g asparagus contain 20 calories.

Tip
■ Asparagus is delicate and perishable and should be used as soon as possible after purchase.

To Prepare Asparagus

White asparagus should be peeled or scraped before cooking. The peeling should start at the end and gradually become very thin towards the tip.

The green variety does not have to be peeled, but its white end has to be cut off. Wash the asparagus thoroughly, as the tips often contain sand.

To Cook Asparagus

Tie the asparagus in bundles of 10 to 12 with kitchen string. In a deep, stainless steel or enamel pan cook the asparagus in plenty of boiling salted water to cover for 8 to 10 minutes, or until it is tender, but not limp. Transfer it by the strings to a colander and let it drain.

Refresh it under running cold water and gently pat it dry with kitchen paper towel.

ASPARAGUS AU BEURRE
Asparagus With Butter

Simple and delicious. My favourite way of eating asparagus.

2 lb/900 g asparagus
12 tablespoons hot melted butter
salt and freshly ground black pepper

Prepare and cook the asparagus according to directions on page 27.
Just before serving, put the asparagus in a warmed serving dish and pour the butter over. Gently toss, taking care not to break the spears.
Sprinkle with salt and plenty of freshly ground black pepper.
Serve hot on warmed plates.
Serves 4-6

ASPARAGUS WITH HAM VINAIGRETTE

2 lb/900 g asparagus
¼ lb/125 g Prosciutto or Westphalian ham, thinly sliced
3 eggs, hard-boiled and sliced
1 egg, hard-boiled and sieved
3 tomatoes, peeled and sliced

for the dressing
¾ teaspoon salt
¾ teaspoon sugar
¾ teaspoon white pepper
3 tablespoons Dijon mustard
3 tablespoons white wine vinegar
4 tablespoons vegetable oil
4 tablespoons olive oil
3 tablespoons fresh parsley, chopped
1 small gherkin, chopped
2 tablespoons onion, chopped

Prepare and cook the asparagus according to directions on page 27.
Divide the asparagus among 6 salad plates. Arrange the ham,

the egg slices (reserving the smaller slices for the dressing) and the tomato slices on the plates.

In a small bowl blend the salt, sugar, pepper, mustard and vinegar. In a slow stream, whisking constantly, add the olive and the vegetable oil. Whisk the dressing until it emulsifies.

Add the parsley, gherkin, onion and the sieved hard-boiled egg. Whisk again until well blended.

Serve the dressing separately in a sauce-boat. Serve both the asparagus and the dressing very cold.

Serves 6

ASPARAGUS WITH SHERRY VINAIGRETTE

2 lb/900 g asparagus

for the dressing
2 tablespoons Dijon mustard
1 teaspoon sweet paprika
¼ teaspoon cayenne pepper
3 tablespoons white wine vinegar
2 tablespoons medium dry sherry
salt
¼ pint/150 ml olive oil
1 stalk celery, finely chopped
1 tablespoon fresh parsley, finely chopped

Prepare and cook the asparagus according to directions on page 27. Let the asparagus cool.

In a small glass or wooden bowl whisk together the mustard, paprika, cayenne pepper, vinegar, sherry and salt.

Add the oil in a slow stream, whisking vigorously until the dressing emulsifies.

Stir in the celery and parsley. Chill, covered, for at least 2 hours.

Divide the asparagus among 6 chilled plates. Stir the chilled dressing and pour about 2 tablespoons over each serving.

Transfer the remaining dressing to a sauce-boat.

Serve chilled.

Serves 6

ASPARAGUS WITH HAM

2 lb/900 g asparagus
4 large slices boiled ham, thinly cut
1 egg, hard-boiled and chopped
2 teaspoons fresh parsley, finely chopped
¼ pt/150 ml French dressing see page 265

Prepare and cook the asparagus according to directions on page 27. Allow to cool.
Roll 1 or 2 asparagus spears, according to their size, in a quarter piece of ham.
Arrange the rolls on a serving platter.
Mix the egg and the parsley with some French dressing.
Serve the dressing separately in a sauce-boat.
Serve the asparagus and ham very cold.
Serves 4-6

ASPARAGUS WITH CRAB

2 lb/900 g asparagus
2 eggs, hard-boiled and chopped
1 tin crabmeat, drained
¼ pint/150 ml French dressing, see page 265

Prepare and cook the asparagus according to directions on page 27. Mix the egg with some of the dressing.
Arrange the asparagus on a flattish platter. Drizzle the dressing mixed with the eggs over the asparagus.
Decorate the edge of the platter with crabmeat. Serve the remaining dressing in a sauce-boat.
Serve cold.
Serves 4

ASPARAGUS SALAD

16 large asparagus spears
crisp lettuce leaves
1 small cucumber, peeled and sliced
3 eggs, hard-boiled and sliced
1 bunch radishes, cleaned and sliced
mayonnaise, see page 266

Prepare and cook the asparagus according to directions on page 27.
Let it cool, then trim it so that it is entirely edible.
Place 4 spears on 4 plates, which have been lined with lettuce leaves.
Garnish each plate with cucumber, egg and radish slices.
Serve the mayonnaise separately.
Serve cold.
Serves 4

ASPARAGUS À LA POLONAISE

Thick white asparagus is more suitable for this recipe.

2 lb/900 g asparagus
2 eggs, hard-boiled
2 teaspoons parsley, chopped
1 oz/25 g butter
1 oz/25 g toasted breadcrumbs
salt and freshly ground black pepper

Prepare and cook the asparagus according to directions on page 27.
Meanwhile divide the yolks and whites of the eggs. Chop them separately and mix with the parsley.
Heat the butter until slightly browned. Stir in the breadcrumbs.
Heat and stir until the breadcrumbs are slightly browned.
Arrange the well drained asparagus on a warm platter.
Cover the tips with the egg and parsley mixture and buttered breadcrumbs. Add salt and pepper to taste.
Serve hot.
Serves 4

ASPARAGUS PARMIGIANA

2 lb/900 g asparagus
2½ oz/50 g unsalted butter, melted
salt and freshly ground black pepper
1 oz/25 g Parmesan cheese, freshly grated
2 oz/50 g Prosciutto ham, shredded

Prepare and cook the asparagus according to directions on page 27.
Arrange the asparagus in a large gratin or ovenproof dish.
Pour over the butter, sprinkle with salt and pepper.
Toss well, then sprinkle with Parmesan.
Put the dish under the grill, about 5-6 inches/20 cm from the heat, for about 3 minutes, or until the cheese is golden and bubbling.
Sprinkle with shredded Prosciutto.
Serve hot on warm plates.
Serves 4-6

QUICK ICED ASPARAGUS SOUP

This is an ideal recipe for people who don't have time to prepare soups.

2 (about 15 oz/425 g) tins asparagus soup
1 (15 fl oz/142 ml) carton single cream
2 tablespoons onion, finely chopped
1 tomato, peeled, cut into small pieces

In a large bowl combine the soup from the 2 tins. Stir in the cream and mix well.
Chill, covered, for several hours.
Place 1 teaspoon of finely chopped onion and a few pieces of tomato in each chilled soup bowl. Pour in the soup.
Serve chilled.
Serves 4-6

ASPARAGUS SOUP

2 lb/900 g asparagus
3½ pints/2 litres water
1 oz/25 g butter
1 tablespoon flour
pinch of nutmeg
salt and white pepper
2 egg yolks
½ pint/300 ml double cream
1 tablespoon fresh chives, finely chopped

Trim the ends of the asparagus, and cut into 1 inch/2.5 cm segments.

Cook the asparagus in boiling salted water until very tender. Drain, but reserve the stock.

In a heavy saucepan melt the butter, stir in the flour and slowly add the asparagus stock, stirring constantly. Add the nutmeg, salt and pepper to taste.

Cook the mixture for several minutes, uncovered, stirring frequently.

Add the asparagus segments and reduce the heat. Cook for a further 5 minutes, stirring from time to time.

Mix the cream with the egg yolks, add a little more pepper and pour it into the soup just before serving.

Sprinkle each portion with chopped chives.

Serve hot in warm soup plates or bowls.

Serves 6

ASPARAGUS MOUSSE

¾ pint/450 ml boiling water
3 level teaspoons powdered gelatine
¾ pint/450 ml single cream
2 egg yolks
1 level teaspoon paprika
½ level teaspoon salt
1 tablespoon lemon juice
6 oz/175 g tinned asparagus tips, drained
and finely chopped
2 egg whites
4 asparagus tips for garnish

Sprinkle the gelatine into boiling water. Stir until it is completely dissolved. Leave until lukewarm.

Warm the cream and beat in the egg yolks. Add it to the dissolved gelatine. Stir in the paprika, salt and lemon juice.

When the mixture is cold and beginning to thicken, stir in the chopped and drained asparagus.

Beat the egg whites until stiff and gently fold them into the asparagus mixture.

Spoon the asparagus mixture into 4 individual bowls, decorate with asparagus spears and chill for several hours. Serve chilled.

Serves 4

Aubergine

The aubergine – or eggplant as it is known outside Britain – is a fruit originating from India. Like so many fruit and vegetables, they were introduced to the New World by Spanish explorers. Mediterranean areas have cultivated the aubergine since the seventeenth century.

There are a number of varieties of this plant: the long purple, the round purple, the giant New York, the Chinese aubergine and small ivory coloured aubergines, which bear a close resemblance to eggs.

Although low in calories, most recipes seem to require a certain amount of oils and fats, which negate this advantage. The aubergine is fairly tasteless, but this can be overcome by the additional use of garlic, onions and lemons.

4 oz/100 g of aubergine contain 25 calories. It is high in vitamins B, C, calcium and iron.

Tips
■ Aubergines contain bitter juice and to remove it the aubergine must be salted and left standing to drain for 15-30 minutes.

■ Aubergines must be firm and even in colour. If soft and shrivelled they should be avoided as they have been stored for too long.

STUFFED AUBERGINE

4 small aubergines, cut lengthwise
3 onions, finely chopped
4 tablespoons olive oil
4 oz/100 g mushrooms, chopped
4 tablespoons fresh parsley, chopped
3½ oz/100 g toasted breadcrumbs
2 egg yolks
salt and freshly ground black pepper

Spoon out most of the flesh of the aubergines, leaving only a thin layer next to the skin. Set aside.
Sprinkle the aubergine halves with salt. Leave to drain, flesh side down. Chop the reserved flesh.
Cook the onions in half of the oil until lightly browned.
Mix in the chopped aubergine and cook, stirring, until the moisture has completely evaporated. Add the mushrooms, the parsley and enough breadcrumbs to make a firm mixture. Season with salt and pepper.
Remove from the heat and stir in the egg yolks.
Pat the aubergine shells dry. Fill them with this mixture.
Dust the tops with the remaining breadcrumbs. Arrange the aubergines in a baking dish large enough to hold them in one layer.
Sprinkle with the remaining oil and cook in a preheated oven (350°F/180°C/Gas Mark 4) for 45 minutes.
Serve hot.
Serves 4

FRIED AUBERGINE STICKS

As the aubergine has to be deep fried and served immediately,
it is a more suitable starter for an informal meal with
a small number of people.

1 aubergine, about 1 lb/450 g
seasoned flour
6 fl oz/150 ml evaporated milk
4 oz/100 g toasted breadcrumbs

oil for deep frying
parsley, finely chopped

Peel the aubergine and cut it into narrow sticks. Sprinkle with salt and let them drain for 30 minutes.

Pat the aubergine sticks dry and dust them with well-seasoned flour.

In two separate dishes have ready the milk and the breadcrumbs.

Dip the aubergine sticks in the milk, letting excess drip off, then dredge with the breadcrumbs.

Chill the sticks for 30 minutes. Deep fry them in the oil, turning from time to time, until they are golden brown.

Transfer them with a slotted spoon onto absorbent kitchen paper towels to drain.

Arrange the aubergine sticks on a platter and sprinkle with parsley.

Serve hot.
Serves 4

AUBERGINE SALAD

1 aubergine, about 1 lb/450 g
vegetable oil for shallow frying
1 clove of garlic, peeled
1 tablespoon fresh lemon juice
salt and freshly ground black pepper

Peel and slice the aubergine. Sprinkle with salt and leave to drain for 30 minutes.

Drain off water and pat dry. Shallow fry the slices in hot oil until brown on both sides. Drain off the fat on absorbent kitchen paper.

Put the aubergine slices, garlic, lemon juice, salt and pepper into an electric blender or mixer and blend until smooth. Check the seasoning.

Place into ramekin dishes. Chill, covered, for several hours.

Serve chilled.
Serves 4

BAKED MARINATED AUBERGINE

4 aubergines, about 8 oz/225 g each
¼ pint/450 ml French dressing, see page 265
3 oz/75 g fresh basil, chopped
3 oz/75 g fresh parsley, chopped
1 onion, chopped
4 cloves of garlic, crushed
3-4 tablespoons lemon juice
1 teaspoon ground coriander
1 teaspoon ground cumin
1 teaspoon salt
freshly ground black pepper
chopped parsley for garnish

Cut the aubergines in half lengthwise and score the cut sides diagonally.

Arrange the aubergines, cut sides up, in an ovenproof dish large enough to hold them in one layer.

Pour over the French dressing and bake in a preheated oven (400°F/200°C/Gas Mark 6) for 30 minutes. Cool them, still in the dressing, then transfer with a slotted spoon to a cutting board. Reserve the dressing.

Scoop out the pulp, leaving ¼ inch/0.5 cm thick shells.

In an electric blender or mixer blend the aubergine pulp, basil, parsley, ¼ pint/150 ml of the reserved dressing, onion, garlic, lemon juice, coriander, cumin and salt and pepper to taste.

Divide the mixture between the aubergine shells. Arrange them in one layer in another baking dish. Pour 2 tablespoons of the reserved French dressing over the aubergines.

Return them to the oven (400°F/200°C/Gas Mark 6) for 25 minutes.

Cool, then chill for at least 6 hours, covered.

With a slotted spoon transfer the chilled aubergines to individual serving plates. Sprinkle with chopped parsley.

Serve cold.

Serves 8

AUBERGINE WITH CAPERS

1 large aubergine, cut into small cubes
3 tablespoons olive oil
1 clove of garlic, crushed
1 onion, thinly sliced
4 stalks of celery, chopped
1½ tablespoons tomato purée
4 tablespoons capers
12 black olives, pitted and chopped
6 green stuffed olives, chopped
2 tablespoons white wine vinegar
1 tablespoon sugar
salt and freshly ground black pepper
lemon wedges
water

Sprinkle the aubergine cubes with salt and let them drain for 15-30 minutes. Pat them dry.

In a heavy saucepan heat 2 tablespoons of the olive oil and sauté the cubes until they begin to get soft.

With a slotted spoon remove them from the pan and set aside.

Sauté the garlic and the onion in the third tablespoon of olive oil until the onion turns golden. Add the celery, the tomato purée and a few tablespoons of water. Stir well, then cover the pan and let it simmer very gently for 10-15 minutes, stirring occasionally. Add a little more water if required.

Return the aubergine cubes to the pan, add the capers and the olives.

In a separate pan, heat the vinegar with the sugar, then add it to the aubergine mixture. Simmer gently for another 10-15 minutes, stirring occasionally.

Add salt and pepper to taste.

Cool, then chill it in the refrigerator for several hours.

Serve chilled with wedges of lemon.

Serves 6-8

AUBERGINE SESAME

1 large aubergine
1 clove of garlic, crushed
3 tablespoons sour cream
¾ teaspoon salt
1 teaspoon lemon juice
cayenne pepper
freshly ground black pepper
2½ tablespoons sesame seeds

Prick the aubergine with a fork a few times and place it in a preheated oven (375°F/190°C/Gas Mark 5). Bake for an hour, or until the flesh is soft to the touch. Let it cool, then scoop out the pulp. Discard the skin and mash the pulp well. Add the garlic, salt, lemon juice, sour cream, cayenne pepper and plenty of freshly ground black pepper. Blend well.
Roast the sesame seeds either in a small pan or in a hot oven (400°F/200°C/Gas Mark 6) until they are slightly brown. Let them cool a little, then stir half of them into the aubergine mixture. Turn the mixture into a serving dish and sprinkle with the remaining seeds.
Serve chilled with bread-sticks or Melba toast.
Serves 4

AUBERGINES WITH CHEESE

2 large aubergines
8 oz/225 g cottage cheese
2 cloves of garlic, crushed
2 spring onions, chopped
1 green pepper, chopped
8 black olives, pitted and chopped
3 tablespoons olive oil
2 tablespoons lemon juice
salt and freshly ground black pepper
1 teaspoon parsley, chopped
lettuce leaves, shredded

Prick the aubergines with a fork a few times and place them in the oven (450°F/230°C/Gas Mark 8) until the skins are black and the flesh feels soft to the touch.

When cool enough to handle, peel off the skins. Put the flesh into a large bowl and mash it with a fork.

In a separate bowl mash the cottage cheese, then add it to the aubergine. Blend in the garlic, onions, pepper and olives. Mix well; add the oil, lemon juice, salt and pepper to taste. Combine the mixture well.

Line individual bowls or plates with the shredded lettuce. Arrange the aubergine mixture in the middle and sprinkle it with chopped parsley. Chill for at least 1 hour.

Serve chilled with pitta or French bread.

Serves 6

AUBERGINE CAVIAR

6 tablespoons olive oil
1 onion, finely chopped
2 cloves of garlic, crushed
1 green pepper, seeded and chopped
1 large aubergine, peeled and finely chopped
3 tomatoes, peeled, seeded and finely chopped
½ teaspoon sugar
freshly ground black pepper
1½ teaspoons salt, or according to taste
2 tablespoons fresh lemon juice
crisp lettuce leaves
chopped parsley for garnish

In a heavy saucepan heat the oil and cook the onion, garlic and pepper, stirring, until all the vegetables are softened.

Add the aubergine and continue cooking over moderate heat for 20 minutes. Stir frequently.

Add the tomatoes, sugar, salt and pepper to taste. Cook over low heat, stirring frequently, for a further 45 minutes, or until it is the consistency of a coarse purée. Remove the pan from the heat; stir in the lemon juice. Check the seasoning.

Chill, covered, for at least 6 hours or overnight.

Serve cold on individual plates lined with lettuce leaves. Sprinkle with finely chopped parsley.

Serves 4

Avocado

'A large pear-shaped fruit also called "alligator pear".' (Shorter Oxford Dictionary)

Reputedly there are 400 different kinds of avocados, some of them the size of a plum, others weighing up to one kilo. The avocados which reach our shops are shaped like pears or apples with light to dark green – or aubergine to nearly black – skins. The texture of the skin also varies from smooth to rough.

The creamy flesh of the avocado is fairly bland in taste and, consequently, suitable for a great number of starters.

High in vitamins A and B, the avocado is also high in calories. 1 oz/25 g of avocado flesh contains 24 calories.

Tips
■ Ripe avocados can be stored in the refrigerator for 4-6 days.
■ Unripe avocados will ripen on a sunny window-sill or in a warm place.
■ Once opened, the flesh should be sprinkled with lemon juice immediately to avoid discolouration.

AVOCADO VINAIGRETTE

2 ripe avocados
4 large tablespoons French dressing, see page 265
finely chopped parsley or chives

Cut the avocados in half with a stainless steel knife.
Remove the stones and fill the hollows with French dressing.
Sprinkle with chopped parsley or chives.
Serve immediately.
Serves 4

AVOCADO AND GRAPEFRUIT

2 ripe avocados
1 large grapefruit, peeled and cut into segments
2 tablespoons sultanas
washed leaves of 2 lettuces
¼ pint/150 ml French dressing, see page 265
2 tablespoons almonds, chopped

Mix the grapefruit segments with the sultanas and the
lettuce leaves.
Add the French dressing; toss well.
Cut the avocados in half with a stainless steel knife. Peel, and
remove the stones. Cut the halves into thin slices. Place
them on the grapefruit and lettuce mixture.
Toss very gently, or the avocados will make the salad mushy.
Sprinkle with almonds.
Serve immediately.
Serves 4-6

AVOCADO WITH GRAPES

3 ripe avocados
1 lb/450 g dark grapes, halved and seeded
1 tablespoon lemon juice
2 stalks celery, finely chopped
1 teaspoon fresh lime juice
1 tablespoon unsweetened pineapple juice
¼ pint/150 ml red wine
1½ tablespoons castor sugar
salt
cayenne pepper
fresh mint

With a stainless steel knife cut the avocados in half and remove the stones. Brush the avocados with lemon juice and sprinkle with a little salt.
Combine the grapes and the celery. Spoon the mixture into the hollows of the avocados.
Blend together the lime juice, pineapple juice, wine, sugar and cayenne pepper.
Spoon the dressing over the avocados. Garnish with mint. Serve chilled.
Serves 6

AVOCADOS WITH ONION VINAIGRETTE

2 ripe avocados

for the dressing
3 tablespoons red wine vinegar
salt
1 teaspoon Dijon mustard
pinch of sugar
freshly ground black pepper
6 tablespoons olive oil
3 tablespoons onion, finely grated

In a small bowl whisk the vinegar with the salt, mustard, sugar and pepper. Add the oil in a slow stream, whisking, until the dressing emulsifies.

Stir in the onion and whisk again.

Cut the avocados in half with a stainless steel knife. peel and remove the stones. Cut the avocado halves into thin slices. Arrange them on a platter and drizzle over the onion dressing.

Serve immediately.

Serves 4-6

AVOCADO AND BACON COCKTAIL

3 ripe avocados
4 tablespoons mayonnaise, see page 266
2 tablespoons tomato ketchup
2 tablespoons lemon juice
2 tablespoons fresh orange juice
few drops tabasco sauce
2 tablespoons celery, finely chopped
2 tablespoons spring onion tops, chopped
5 rashers bacon, grilled and crumbled
salt and freshly ground black pepper

Mix the mayonnaise with the ketchup, lemon juice, orange juice, tabasco sauce and salt and pepper to taste.

In a large bowl mix the celery with the spring onion tops.

With a stainless steel knife cut the avocados in half, peel and remove stones, then dice the halves. Add the diced avocado to the celery and spring onion mixture. Toss gently. Spoon the mayonnaise mixture over it and mix carefully.

Chill for 30 minutes, then serve in chilled bowls or cocktail glasses. Sprinkle each serving with crisp bacon bits.

Serves 6

AVOCADO AND CELERY COCKTAIL

2 ripe avocados
4 tablespoons tomato ketchup
2 tablespoons fresh lemon juice
½ tablespoon onion, finely grated
½ teaspoon prepared horseradish sauce
¼ teaspoon cayenne pepper
salt to taste
pinch of sugar
2 tablespoons celery, finely chopped

Blend together the ketchup, lemon juice, onion, horse-
radish, cayenne, salt and sugar.
Chill, covered, for at least 1 hour.
With a stainless steel knife cut the avocados in half, and peel
and stone them.
Cut the halves into ½ inch/1 cm cubes and mix with the
celery.
Spoon the mixture into 4-6 individual bowls or cocktail
glasses.
Pour over the chilled sauce.
Serve immediately.
Serves 4-6

AVOCADO WITH STILTON AND CREAM DRESSING

*The Stilton adds a special touch to the cream dressing. Delicious, but
rich! The following course should be fairly light.*

3 ripe avocados

for the dressing
3 oz/75 g Stilton, crumbled
¼ pint/150 ml single cream
2 tablespoons vegetable oil
juice of 1 lemon
1 teaspoon Worcestershire sauce
half a small onion, finely grated
1 tablespoon parsley, chopped
salt and pepper

In a bowl beat the Stilton with the cream until smooth. Add the oil, lemon juice, Worcestershire sauce, onion and parsley. Blend well and season with salt and pepper.
With a stainless steel knife cut the avocados in half and remove the stones.
Spoon the Stilton dressing into the hollow of the avocados. Serve immediately.
Serves 6

AVOCADO CHICKEN SALAD

4 ripe avocados
juice of 1 lemon
2 oz/50 g cooked chicken, diced
2 tablespoons celery, chopped
2 tablespoons cucumber, peeled, seeded and chopped
2 tablespoons fresh parsley, chopped
¼ pint/450 g double cream
½ oz/15 g toasted almonds, slivered
salt and freshly ground white pepper
chopped parsley for garnish
paprika

With a stainless steel knife cut the avocados in half and remove the stones. Without piercing the skins, remove some of the flesh, leaving about ½ inch/0.5 cm in the shell.
Sprinkle the shells with lemon juice.
Dice the avocado flesh and sprinkle it with lemon juice.
In a large bowl combine the chicken, celery, cucumber, parsley and cream. Mix well, add a little lemon juice, salt and pepper.
Add the avocado dice: blend them in carefully, or they will make the salad mushy.
Sprinkle in the almonds. Fill the empty shells with the chicken mixture. Dust with paprika and sprinkle with chopped parsley.
Serves 8

AVOCADOS STUFFED WITH CRAB

3 ripe avocados
1 tin crabmeat
French dressing, see page 265
6 crisp lettuce leaves
juice of half a lemon
paprika

With a stainless steel knife cut the avocados in half and remove the stones. Without piercing the skins, carefully remove some of the flesh, leaving about ¼ inch/0.5 cm in the shell.

Dice the avocado flesh. Sprinkle the shells with lemon juice to avoid discolouration.

Drain the crabmeat and mix carefully with the avocado cubes.

Spoon over the French dressing and pile the mixture back into the empty shells.

Arrange each avocado half on a lettuce leaf. Dust with paprika.

Serves 6

GUACAMOLE

I first had this piquant starter when travelling through Mexico many years ago. Since then 'guacamole' has become an internationally known speciality.

2 large ripe avocados
half a small onion, finely chopped
2 tomatoes, peeled and finely chopped
1 small green pepper, seeded and chopped
1 clove of garlic, crushed
juice of 1 small lemon
1 tablespoon olive oil
dash of tabasco sauce
salt and freshly ground black pepper
crisp lettuce leaves

Beetroot Sorbet (see page 68) and, on the right, *Celery and Apple Sorbet* (see page 74) – cool and refreshing on hot summer days.

Minted Grape and Melon Cocktail (see page 158) is a light starter which can be followed by a rich main course.

Cucumber and Yoghurt Mousse, above left, is an ideal starter for summer (see page 98).

Below left: *Avocados Stuffed with Crab* (see page 48); a starter for all occasions.

Mozzarella and Tomato Salad (see page 85). A typical Italian starter which can be
prepared at the last minute.

With a stainless steel knife cut the avocados in half, remove the stones and scoop out all the flesh. Discard the shells.
Mash the flesh with a wooden spoon or a silver fork until smooth. Sprinkle with lemon juice.
In a large bowl combine the onion, tomatoes, pepper, garlic and olive oil. Add the mashed avocados and mix well.
Add the remaining lemon juice, tabasco, salt and plenty of freshly ground black pepper. Blend well.
Serve on individual plates or in bowls lined with lettuce.
Serve cold.
Serves 4-6

BAKED AVOCADO HALVES

*Although I first sampled this dish on a hot evening in California,
I think it makes an excellent winter starter.*

2 ripe avocados
1 egg white
4 tablespoons mayonnaise, see page 266
pinch of curry powder
salt and freshly ground white pepper
crisp lettuce leaves

With a stainless steel knife cut the avocados in half, remove the stones and peel.
Place the avocados pitted side upwards in a slightly greased baking dish.
Beat the egg white until stiff, then fold it into the mayonnaise. Add curry powder, salt and pepper.
Pile the mixture into the hollows of the avocados. Bake in a moderate oven (350°F/180°C/Gas Mark 4) for several minutes, or until the meringue is slightly browned.
Place on plates lined with a lettuce leaf. Serve immediately.
Serves 4

BAKED AVOCADO WITH CURRIED CRAB

3 ripe avocados
1 tablespoon fresh lemon juice
1 tin crabmeat, drained
4 tablespoons celery, chopped
2 tablespoons spring onion, thinly sliced
1 tablespoon fruit chutney
2 teaspoons curry powder
pinch of cayenne pepper
1 egg yolk
½ pint/300 ml mayonnaise, see page 266
sprigs of parsley

With a stainless steel knife cut the avocados in half, remove the stones and peel. Brush the halves with a little lemon juice.

Arrange them, pitted side upwards, in a slightly greated baking dish. Bake them in a preheated oven (350°F/180°C/ Gas Mark 4) for 10 minutes.

Combine the crabmeat, celery, spring onion, fruit chutney, curry powder, cayenne, egg yolk, half of the mayonnaise and the remaining lemon juice. Mix well.

Pile the crab mixture into the hollow parts of the avocados, top with the remaining mayonnaise and put under the grill about 6 inches/25 cm) from the heat for 3 minutes, or until the topping is golden.

Transfer the avocados to separate plates. Garnish with sprigs of parsley.

Serve immediately.

Serves 6

AVOCADO MOUSSE

2 large ripe avocados
1 (0.4 oz/11 g) envelope powdered gelatine
½ pint/300 ml chicken stock
1 tablespoon fresh lemon juice
¼ pint/150 ml double cream
¼ pint/150 ml mayonnaise, see page 266
salt and freshly ground white pepper
dash of tabasco sauce
1 teaspoon Worcestershire sauce
pinch of celery salt
sprigs of watercress for garnish

Soften the gelatine in a little stock. Heat the rest of the stock and pour it into the gelatine.

With a stainless steel knife cut the avocados in half, peel and remove stones. Mash the avocados with a wooden spoon or a silver fork until smooth. Sprinkle with lemon juice.

Whip the cream lightly. Fold it, together with the mayonnaise, into the avocado mixture. Add salt, pepper, tabasco, Worcestershire sauce and celery salt. Mix well.

As soon as the stock is beginning to set, beat it into the avocado mixture and pour it into a rinsed mould.

Chill for several hours, or until set.

To turn out, dip the mould briefly into hot water, then run a pointed knife blade round the edge of the mousse. Invert a serving plate over the top, and turn the dish and the plate over together. Give a sharp shake to dislodge the mousse.

Garnish with watercress sprigs.

Serve chilled.

Serves 4-6

AVOCADO AND PRAWN MOUSSE

3 ripe avocados
8 oz/225 g cream cheese
¼ pint/150 ml natural yoghurt
1 tablespoon lemon juice
6 drops tabasco sauce
1 small onion, chopped
pinch of celery salt
salt and freshly ground white pepper
4 oz/100 g prawns, cooked and peeled
paprika
chopped parsley

In a bowl combine the cheese, yoghurt, lemon juice, tabasco, onion, celery salt, salt and freshly ground white pepper. Cover and leave to stand for 3-4 hours.
With a stainless steel knife cut the avocados in half and remove the stones. Scoop out the flesh, discarding the shells. Mash the flesh with the cheese mixture and blend until smooth. Add the prawns and mix.
Serve immediately on chilled plates. Sprinkle each serving with parsley and dust with paprika.
Serves 4-6

AVOCADO WITH MUSHROOM AND BRANDY

2 firm but ripe avocados
juice of half a lemon
2 tablespoons dried imported mushrooms
2 oz/50 g butter
8 oz/225 g fresh mushrooms, sliced
1 tablespoon brandy
¼ pint/150 ml double cream
1 egg yolk
salt and pepper
chopped parsley

With a stainless steel knife cut the avocados in half and remove the stones. Scoop the flesh from the avocados with a

52

melon-ball cutter, leaving ¼ inch/0.5 cm in the shells.
Arrange the shells on 4 individual plates and brush them
with some of the lemon juice.
Soak the dried mushrooms in hot water for 10-15 minutes.
Drain, and cook them in the butter over moderate heat for
about 3 minutes, stirring occasionally. Add the fresh
mushrooms and cook for a further 2 minutes. Add the
brandy and the cream and heat through without boiling.
In a small bowl whisk the egg yolk with 2 tablespoons of the
liquid from the mushrooms and return it to the remaining
mushroom mixture.
Simmer it over low heat until it thickens slightly.
Add the avocado balls, stir gently and heat through.
Add the lemon juice, salt and pepper and spoon the mixture
into the avocado shells. Garnish with parsley. Serve while hot.
Serves 4

COLD AVOCADO SOUP

1¼ pt/750 ml cold chicken stock
1 large ripe avocado
salt to taste
1 (5 fl oz/142 ml) carton single cream
1 tablespoon medium dry sherry
½ teaspoon lemon juice
pinch of sugar
freshly ground black pepper
fresh chives, chopped

With a stainless steel knife cut the avocado in half, remove
the stone and peel. Scoop out all the flesh and cut it into
small pieces. Discard the shells.
Place the avocado pieces, the salt and the chicken stock into
an electric blender or mixer and blend until smooth.
Pour into a bowl and chill, covered, for several hours.
Mix the cream with the sherry, lemon juice, sugar and
freshly ground black pepper. Chill this mixture in a separate
container and add to the soup just before serving. Stir well.
Garnish with chopped chives. Serve in chilled soup bowls.
Serves 4

AVOCADO AND POTATO CREAM

*A velvety creamy dish. But be generous with the black pepper
as both the avocado and the potato are fairly bland.*

1 ripe avocado
8 oz/225 g potatoes
1 oz/25 g butter
1 clove of garlic, crushed
4 tablespoons double cream
pinch of nutmeg
salt and freshly ground black pepper
crisp lettuce leaves
chopped fresh chives or parsley

Peel the potatoes and cut them into large dice. Boil them in
salted water until tender, but not mushy.
Drain and, while still warm, blend in the butter and mash the
potatoes.
With a stainless steel knife, halve and stone the avocado.
Scoop out the flesh and mash it with a wooden spoon or a
silver fork, until it is smooth. Combine it with the mashed
potatoes and mix well.
Season with salt, pepper and nutmeg and stir in the crushed
garlic and the cream. Mix well and chill, covered, for several
hours.
Sprinkle with chopped chives or parsley.
Serve cold on chilled plates lined with crisp lettuce leaves.
Serves 4

Beans

For centuries beans have provided food for most countries. According to archaeologists the broad bean, one of the oldest beans, was cultivated by prehistoric man. The Romans regarded beans as unlucky, and the harmless broad bean was linked with death. Although dried beans were not a part of the Roman diet, they were used in voting in elections, the white bean being 'for', the black 'against'. Beans supplied the main source of protein for the Aztecs when Cortez discovered Mexico in 1519.

There are many species, including the string bean from South America. The kidney bean, originated in Peru and grown in other parts of South America before it was established in France, finally came to England before the end of the Elizabethan reign.

Apart from large butter beans and the smaller haricot, dried beans were not very popular in England until very recently.

Butter and Lima beans are high in potassium, vitamin B and iron.
Broad beans are high in vitamin B and C and potassium.
Green beans are high in potassium and vitamin C.
Red beans contain potassium and vitamins B and C.

4 oz/100 g of most dried beans contain 352 calories.
4 oz/100 g of green beans contain 33 calories.

GREEN BEANS VINAIGRETTE

1 lb/450 g French green beans
1½ oz/40 g Parmesan cheese, grated
1 small onion, finely chopped
1 clove of garlic, crushed

for the dressing
2 tablespoons tarragon vinegar
½ teaspoon Dijon mustard
1 teaspoon fresh tarragon, chopped OR
½ teaspoon dried tarragon
salt and freshly ground black pepper
pinch of sugar
6 tablespoons olive oil

Wash the beans, snip off the ends, and cut them into 1 inch/ 2.5 cm pieces. Boil in salted water until just tender but still crisp. Drain, refresh under running cold water and sprinkle with Parmesan. Add the onion and the garlic.
In a small bowl whisk the vinegar, salt, mustard, tarragon, sugar and plenty of freshly ground black pepper. Add the oil in a slow stream and whisk until the dressing emulsifies.
Pour the dressing over the beans, which should be still warm. Check the seasoning and toss the salad well.
Chill, covered, for about 1 hour.
Serves 4

BEAN SALAD WITH WALNUTS

1½ lb/675 g French green beans
3 tablespoons white wine vinegar
1 teaspoon Dijon mustard
salt and freshly ground black pepper
1 clove of garlic, crushed
6 tablespoons olive oil
2 oz/50 g walnuts, chopped
1 tablespoon fresh parsley, finely chopped

Wash the beans, snip off the ends, and boil them in salted water until tender but still crisp.

In a small bowl whisk the vinegar with the mustard, salt and pepper and garlic. Slowly add the olive oil, whisking, until the dressing emulsifies.

Drain the beans, refresh under running cold water and pour the dressing over the still warm beans.

Sprinkle with walnuts and parsley. Toss well.

Chill for 2-3 hours, covered.

Serves 4-6

GREEN BEANS WITH HORSERADISH DRESSING

The tangy taste of horseradish adds zest to this excellent summer starter.

1 lb/450 g fresh French green beans
1 tablespoon prepared horseradish
½ teaspoon Dijon mustard
2½ tablespoons sour cream
2 tablespoons vegetable oil
4 rashers streaky bacon
salt and pepper

Wash the beans, snip off the ends, and boil in salted water until tender but still crisp.

Drain the beans and refresh under running cold water.

Chill, covered, for at least 1 hour.

In a small bowl, whisk together the horseradish, mustard, oil, sour cream and salt and pepper to taste.

Chill, covered, for at least 1 hour.

Cut the bacon crosswise into ½ inch/1 cm pieces and fry or grill until brown and crisp. Transfer with a slotted spoon to absorbent kitchen paper to drain. Crumble the bacon. Arrange the beans on a chilled serving platter, spoon the dressing over them and sprinkle with the crumbled bacon.

Serve chilled with French bread.

Serves 4

GREEN BEANS IN YOGHURT AND TOMATO SAUCE

1 lb/450 g fresh French green beans
2 oz/50 g butter
1 onion, thinly sliced
1 green pepper, thinly sliced
3 tomatoes, peeled and chopped
2 tablespoons fresh basil, chopped, OR
¾ teaspoon dried basil
1 egg
½ pint/300 ml natural yoghurt
salt and freshly ground black pepper

Wash the beans, snip off the ends, and boil in salted water until tender but still crisp. Drain and refresh under running cold water and set aside.

In a large saucepan melt the butter, add the onion and the green pepper and cook, stirring frequently, until the onion is transparent and the pepper soft.

Add the tomatoes and basil. Cook for a further 5 minutes over moderate heat, stirring constantly.

Add the beans, mixing them well with the other vegetables, and simmer for 5 minutes.

In a separate bowl, beat the egg with the yoghurt and season with salt and plenty of freshly ground black pepper.

Fold the yoghurt mixture into the vegetables. Gently heat through without bringing it to boil.

Serve immediately, sprinkled with chopped parsley and accompanied by pitta or French bread.
Serves 4-6

MARINATED BEAN SALAD

1 lb/450 g fresh French green beans
6 oz/175 g red kidney beans, cooked
6 oz/175 g chick-peas, cooked
1 large onion, thinly cut

for the dressing:
¼ pint/150 ml olive oil
¼ pint/150 ml cider or white wine vinegar

3 tablespoons sugar
1 green pepper, finely chopped
1 tablespoon parsley, finely chopped
salt
plenty of freshly ground black pepper

Combine the green beans, the kidney beans, the chick-peas and the onion in a large bowl.
In a separate bowl whisk the vinegar, the sugar and the black pepper. Add the olive oil in a steady stream, whisking all the time. Add the green pepper, the parsley and the salt.
Mix well and pour the dressing over the bean mixture.
Cover, and chill overnight.
Serve cold accompanied by French or herb bread.

FRENCH BEAN SOUP

2 lb/900 g fresh French green beans
2 oz/50 g butter
1 tablespoon flour
3 tablespoons double cream
1½ pint/900 ml chicken stock
1 tablespoon parsley, chopped
salt to taste
freshly ground black pepper
1 tablespoon lemon juice

Wash the beans, snip off the ends and cut them into 1 inch/ 2.5 cm long pieces.
In a large saucepan combine beans with the chicken stock.
Bring the mixture to the boil without the lid on, then simmer, covered, until the beans are very tender.
In a separate saucepan melt the butter, stir in the flour and the parsley, and slowly pour in the stock with the beans.
Stir until it begins to boil, then simmer gently, with the lid on, for 20-25 minutes.
Add the lemon juice and the cream, but do not boil again.
Correct the seasoning.
Serve hot.
Serves 4-6

BROWN BEAN SOUP

This is a very filling first course.

1 lb/450 g dried brown lentils
2 pints/1.2 litres water
1 bay leaf
2 lb/900 g piece of bacon
2 oz/50 g butter
1 tablespoon flour
salt and freshly ground black pepper

Soak the beans in 2 pints/1.2 litres of water.
Bring to boil in the same water: add the bay leaf and simmer until the beans are soft.
At the same time put the bacon to boil in a separate saucepan with about 1¾ pints/1 litre of water. Simmer the bacon until the beans are ready.
Cool, skim off the fat from the bacon stock and discard. Set the bacon aside.
Melt the butter in a large saucepan and stir in the flour.
Gradually add the bacon stock, stirring constantly, then add the beans with their stock, discarding the bay leaf.
Slice the bacon and add it to the bean soup. Heat thoroughly before serving.
Serves 6

BROAD BEAN SALAD WITH BACON

1 lb/450 g frozen broad beans
8 rashers streaky bacon
4 spring onions, chopped
3 tablespoons French dressing, see page 265
dash of tabasco sauce
salt and pepper
crisp lettuce leaves

Cook the beans according to the instructions. Drain, refresh under cold running water and place them in a bowl. Spoon over the French dressing while the beans are still warm. Mix well and set aside to cool.

Grill or fry the bacon until it is very crisp. Drain it on absorbent kitchen paper, then crumble it.

Mix the onions with the beans, add a few drops of tabasco sauce, and season – according to taste – with salt and pepper. Arrange the bean salad on individual plates or bowls lined with crisp lettuce leaves.

Sprinkle each portion with crumbled bacon. Serve very cold.
Serves 4

BEAN SALAD WITH SMOKED HADDOCK

1 (14½ oz/410 g) tin white haricot beans, drained
1 lb/450 g smoked haddock
a little milk and water
¼ pint/150 ml natural yoghurt
1 tablespoon lemon juice
1 teaspoon mild onion, grated
1 teaspoon curry powder
1 tablespoon parsley, chopped
1 egg, hard-boiled and sliced
1 tablespoon capers (optional)
salt and pepper
crisp lettuce leaves

In a shallow saucepan bring the fish to the boil in just enough water and milk to cover; then simmer for about 10 minutes. Drain well, remove all skin and bones and flake the fish.

In a separate bowl combine the yoghurt, lemon juice, onion and curry powder. Mix well, stir in the fish and the beans. Toss carefully and check the seasoning. Add salt if necessary. Chill, covered, for at least 1 hour.

Serve the salad on individual plates or in bowls, lined with lettuce.

Garnish with egg slices and sprinkle with chopped parsley and chopped capers.
Serves 6

FOUR BEAN SALAD

This recipe from America is an inexpensive and easy-to-prepare starter.

8 oz/225 g fresh French green beans
1 (12 oz/340 g) tin flageolet beans
1 (7½ oz/213 g) tin butter beans
8 oz/225 g broad beans, cooked
1 small onion, finely sliced

for the dressing
2 tablespoons red wine vinegar
1 teaspoon Dijon mustard
1 clove of garlic, crushed
1 tablespoon chives, chopped
1 tablespoon parsley, chopped
1 tablespoon mint, chopped
6 tablespoons vegetable oil
salt and black pepper

Wash the green beans, snip off the ends, and boil them in salted water until tender, but still crisp. Drain, and refresh them under running cold water. Drain the tinned beans and rinse them under cold water to remove the starchy liquid.

In an electric blender or mixer combine the vinegar, mustard, sugar, garlic and herbs. Blend well, then slowly add the oil. Blend until the mixture is well emulsified. Season with salt and freshly ground black pepper.

Pour the dressing over the beans, and stir well. Chill, covered, for at least 2-3 hours.

Serve cold.

Serves 6

Beetroot

The beetroot originates from parts of Asia and Europe and was mainly cultivated in cool regions.

The leaves of the beet are green and edible, but nowadays it is generally grown for its dark-red root. The Romans cultivated it and used its leaves as a vegetable. In Russia, both leaves and root are used a great deal.

It reached England towards the end of the Elizabethan age from Italy or France and was usually boiled and eaten in a salad.

The beetroot is low in calories, contains vitamin A, iron and phosphorus.
4 oz/100 g of beetroot contain 37 calories.

Tip
■ Never cut the beetroot before cooking it, or it will lose its red colouring.

BEETROOT SALAD

6 medium beetroot, cooked
1 small onion, thinly sliced
1 small apple, peeled, cored and chopped
1 tablespoon vinegar
¼ teaspoon caraway seeds
pinch of sugar
salt and freshly ground black pepper
3 tablespoons vegetable oil

Peel and thinly slice the beetroot. Arrange it, on a flat salad platter, mixed with the onion and apple.
In a small bowl blend the vinegar with the caraway seeds, sugar, salt and pepper. Whisk in the oil until the dressing emulsifies.
Pour the dressing over the beetroot and chill, covered, for at least 3 hours.
Serve very cold accompanied by hot French or garlic bread.
Seves 5-8

BEETROOT SALAD WITH WALNUTS

2 heads of chicory (known as 'endive' in Europe and USA)
leaves of 1 small round lettuce, washed and dried
2 large beetroot, cooked and peeled
4 fl oz/100 ml French dressing, see page 265
2 oz/50 g walnuts, chopped

With a sharp, pointed knife cut ¼ inch/0.5 cm off the base of the chicory and scrape out a little of the core.
Cut the heads into 1 inch/2.5 cm diagonal slices.
Wash and pat dry with kitchen paper towel and mix with the lettuce leaves in a large salad bowl.
Just before serving dice the beetroot, add it to the chicory and lettuce and pour the French dressing over.
Sprinkle with chopped walnuts.
Serve cold accompanied by hot herb, garlic or French bread.
Serves 6

BEETROOT WITH ONION AND SOUR CREAM

1½ lb/675 g beetroot, cooked and peeled
1 medium Spanish onion, thinly sliced
4 spring onions, chopped
1 teaspoon lemon juice
1 (5 fl oz/142 ml) carton sour cream
1 teaspoon extra-strong horseradish
¼ teaspoon caraway seeds
pinch of sugar
salt and freshly ground black pepper

Cut the beetroot into thin slices and arrange, together with the sliced onion, in a flat serving dish.
In a bowl blend the sour cream with the horseradish, add the lemon juice, sugar, caraway seeds, salt and pepper.
Spoon the dressing over the beetroot and sprinkle it with the chopped spring onions.
Serve very cold accompanied by French, garlic or herb bread.
Serves 4

BEETROOT WITH PEARS AND WALNUTS IN HORSERADISH DRESSING

4 medium beetroot, cooked and peeled
2 pears, peeled, cored and quartered
2 oz/50 g walnut halves, crumbled
1 tablespoon parsley, finely chopped

for the dressing
5 fl oz/142 ml single cream
1½ teaspoons lemon juice
1 teaspoon extra-strong horseradish
pinch of cayenne
pinch of sugar
salt

Dice the beetroot and the pears, and mix them in a large bowl.

In a separate bowl combine the single cream, horseradish and lemon juice. Whisk and add the cayenne pepper, sugar and salt to taste.

Chill, covered, for at least 3 hours. Sprinkle with chopped parsley and serve very cold accompanied by French or herb bread.

Serves 6

BEETROOT AND CUCUMBER COCKTAIL

1½ lb/675 g beetroot, cooked and peeled
3 cucumbers, peeled, halved and seeded
1 small lettuce, washed and shredded

for the dressing
2 tablespoons lemon juice
1 tablespoon Dijon mustard
¼ teaspoon sugar
6 tablespoons vegetable oil
salt and freshly ground white pepper
3 tablespoons fresh dill, chopped, OR
1 teaspoon dried dill

Cut the beetroot into 2 inch/5 cm by ¼ inch/0.5 cm strips. Slice the peeled and seeded cucumber crosswise into thin rings.

Put the vegetables into separate bowls and chill them for at least 1 hour.

In a separate bowl combine the lemon juice, salt, mustard and sugar and mix well. Slowly add the oil, whisking vigorously until the dressing is smooth. Blend in the dill and pepper to taste.

Just before serving, pour an equal amount of the dressing over the beetroot and the cucumber and toss both vegetables.

Divide the shredded lettuce between 6 chilled salad plates. Mound the beetroot in the centre surrounded by cucumber. Serve chilled with French bread.

Serves 6

BEETROOT SORBET

*Light and refreshing, this inexpensive recipe provides
an ideal summer starter.*

11 oz/300 g beetroot, cooked and peeled
¼ pint/150 ml dry white wine
1 tablespoon green peppercorns
4 teaspoons sour cream
crisp lettuce leaves
fresh chives or spring onion tops, chopped

Chop the beetroot and place it, together with the peppercorns and the white wine, in an electric blender or mixer.
Blend until very smooth, then pour the mixture into a flat
dish and put it into the freezer part of the refrigerator for 2-3
hours.
Stir the mixture from time to time with a fork to prevent the
formation of ice crystals. Line 4 chilled glasses or glass bowls
with lettuce leaves and fill them with the sorbet.
Top each portion with a teaspoon of sour cream, sprinkled
with chives or spring onion tops.
Serve chilled.
Serves 4

BEETROOT WITH HEARTS OF PALM
IN HORSERADISH CREAM

4 small beetroot, cooked and peeled
8 hearts of palm, tinned
crisp lettuce leaves

for the dressing
¼ pint/150 ml double cream
2 tablespoons lemon juice
2 teaspoons extra-strong horseradish sauce
pinch of sugar
salt and white pepper to taste
2 tablespoons olive oil

Line 4 salad plates with the lettuce leaves.
Quarter the beetroot, then slice them about ¼ inch/0.5 cm thick.
Cut the hearts of palm into ½ inch/1 cm rounds.
Divide the palm hearts and the beetroot between the 4 plates, arranging them decoratively.
In a bowl whisk together the cream, lemon juice, horse-radish, sugar, salt and white pepper.
Whisk for 15 seconds, or until the mixture is frothy.
Add the olive oil, drop by drop, as if you were making a mayonnaise. Whisk the dressing until it is well combined, then spoon it over the salad.
Serve cold.
Serves 4

BEETROOT SOUP WITH CABBAGE

This soup is also known as 'bortsch' and is the national soup of Poland and Russia. It makes a tasty winter starter.

1 pint/600 ml chicken stock
2 beetroot, cooked, peeled and grated
2 carrots, grated
2 onions, grated
2 oz/50 g Dutch cabbage, shredded
¼ teaspoon caraway seeds
4 cloves
¼ teaspoon dried marjoram
salt and freshly ground white pepper
1 tablespoon lemon juice
1 (5 fl oz/142 ml) carton sour cream
pinch of sugar

In a large saucepan combine the chicken stock, beetroot, carrots and onions and simmer for 30 minutes.
Add the cabbage, caraway seeds, cloves, marjoram, salt and pepper. Simmer, covered, for a further 25 minutes.
Discard the cloves, add the lemon juice and a pinch of sugar.
Serve hot, each portion topped with sour cream.
Serves 4-6

JELLIED BEETROOT SOUP

4 beetroot, cooked and peeled
2 onions, chopped
2 carrots, chopped
12 black peppercorns
3 sprigs of parsley
1¾ pints/1 litre water
1 lump of sugar
dash of wine vinegar
1½ teaspoons powdered gelatine
salt to taste
1 (5 fl oz/142 ml) carton sour cream
fresh chives, chopped, OR
spring onion tops, chopped
1 teaspoon curry powder

In a large saucepan combine the water, onions, carrots, parsley and peppercorns. Bring to boil, then reduce the heat and simmer, covered, for approximately 1 hour, or until vegetables are soft and have flavoured the stock.
Meanwhile grate the beetroot into a bowl.
Strain the vegetables and discard them. Pour the stock over the beetroot.
Return the beetroot with the stock to the saucepan. Heat, add a lump of sugar, salt and a dash of vinegar. Do not let it boil!
Simmer for 10 minutes over low heat and strain. Discard the grated beetroot.
Soften the gelatine in a teaspoon of hot soup: dissolve thoroughly and add it to the soup. Cool, then chill the soup, covered, in the refrigerator for several hours.
Just before serving, break the jellied soup up with a fork.
Serve in individual chilled bowls with a teaspoon of sour cream, mixed with the curry powder, chopped chives and a little salt.
Serve chilled.
Serves 4-6

BEETROOT AND ORANGE SOUP

1½ pints/900 ml beef stock
1 lb/450 g uncooked beetroot, grated
1 large carrot, chopped
1 large onion, chopped
1 bay leaf
2 cloves
juice and grated rind of 1 orange
¼ pint/150 ml natural yoghurt
salt and freshly ground white pepper

In a large saucepan combine the stock, beetroot, carrot, onion, bay leaf and cloves. Bring to boil; reduce to simmering for 30 minutes.
Remove the bay leaf and the cloves.
Blend the beetroot mixture in an electric blender or mixer until very smooth. Return to the saucepan, add the orange juice and rind and season to taste.
Bring to boil, then reduce heat and slowly stir in the yoghurt.
Heat through, but do not boil or it will curdle.
The soup can be served hot or chilled.
Serves 4

Celery

The Romans harvested this wild plant mainly for medicinal purposes, for it contains an essential oil which is highly aromatic. But they also fed certain kinds of poultry on celery believing that celery gave a special, desirable taste to the poultry flesh.

Celery did not come into cultivation until the sixteenth century. In England, in early times, the wild variety was known as 'smallage', and only in the seventeenth century did Italian gardeners introduce formal cultivation of celery to the English.

To this day, medical-minded folklorists claim that eating celery is a cure for rheumatism.

Celery contains potassium and vitamin B.
4 oz/100 g of celery contain 38 calories.

CELERY À LA GRÈCQUE

3 celery hearts, quartered
¾ pint/450 ml water
3 tablespoons olive oil
3 tablespoons lemon juice
bouquet garni
1 tablespoon black peppercorns
¼ teaspoon coriander seeds
1 medium onion, sliced
salt
chopped parsley for garnish

In a large saucepan combine all the ingredients except the celery hearts.
Bring to the boil, then simmer with the lid on for about 10 minutes.
Add the celery hearts, adding a little more water if they are not covered.
Cook until the celery hearts are tender, but not mushy.
Take them out with a slotted spoon and put them on a serving platter.
Reduce the liquid in the saucepan to a few spoonfuls by fast boiling.
Strain the liquid over the celery hearts.
Cool, then chill, covered, for several hours.
Serve chilled, sprinkled with chopped parsley.
Serves 6

CELERY AND APPLE SORBET

4 stalks of celery, finely chopped
a few celery leaves for garnish
1 shallot, finely chopped
2 apples, peeled, cored and finely chopped
3 tablespoons sauerkraut juice *(available from large
health food or delicatessen shops)*
¼ pint/150 ml white wine
1 egg white

Place the celery, shallot, apples, sauerkraut juice and wine in an electric blender or mixer. Blend until the mixture is smooth, and pour it into a bowl.
Beat the egg white until it is firm but not dry, then fold it into the celery and apple mixture.
Place the bowl in the freezer part of the refrigerator for 2-3 hours. Stir it from time to time with a fork to prevent the formation of icy crystals.
Spoon the sorbet into 4 chilled glasses or small glass bowls and garnish each portion with celery leaves.
Serve chilled with hot triangles of buttered toast.
Serves 4

CELERY VICTOR

2 celery hearts
1 medium onion, sliced
1 pint/600 ml chicken stock
½ pint/300 ml French dressing, see page 265
4 anchovy fillets
4 red pimento strips
shredded lettuce
freshly ground black pepper
chopped parsley

Place the celery hearts and the onion in a shallow saucepan and cover with the chicken stock.
Cook, covered, for 15 minutes, or until hearts are tender.
Cool them in the stock, then remove and cut them in half

lengthwise. Arrange the celery hearts in a shallow platter, spoon over the French dressing and chill for several hours.

Just before serving, line a separate serving dish with the shredded lettuce.

Drain off most of the French dressing, and place the hearts in the dish with the bed of shredded lettuce. Sprinkle with finely chopped parsley and freshly ground black pepper.

Garnish with anchovy fillets and strips of pimento.

Serve very cold.

Serves 4

CELERY SALAD WITH APRICOTS

3 oz/75 g dried apricots
4 tablespoons white wine
3 stalks of celery, finely chopped
2 red apples, cored
1 grapefruit
2 tablespoons sour cream
2 tablespoons natural yoghurt
3 tablespoons mayonnaise, see page 266
salt and freshly ground white pepper
pinch of powdered coriander
2 oz/50 g walnuts, chopped

Soak the apricots in the wine for 30 minutes.

Cut the unpeeled apples into 1 inch/0.2 cm slices.

Peel the grapefruit, divide it into segments and cut each segment into small pieces.

Drain the apricots and reserve the wine. Cut the apricots into thin strips.

In a bowl combine the apricots, celery and apples.

In a separate bowl blend the white wine – in which the apricots were soaked – with the sour cream, mayonnaise, salt, pepper and coriander. Whisk until the sauce is slightly frothy.

Spoon the sauce over the celery mixture and sprinkle with chopped walnuts.

Mix again just before serving. Serve cold on chilled plates.

Serves 4

CELERY AND CARROT SALAD

1 head of celery, finely chopped
3 small carrots, grated
rind and juice of 1 lemon
1 tablespoon vegetable oil
¼ pint/150 ml yoghurt
1 oz/25 g walnuts
¼ teaspoon celery salt
dash of tabasco sauce
pinch of sugar
salt and freshly ground white pepper

In a bowl combine the lemon juice, oil and yoghurt; whisk well, then add the rind, walnuts, celery salt, tabasco and sugar. Whisk again and set aside.
Mix the chopped celery with the grated carrots and add them to the dressing. Toss well and season with salt and pepper. Serve very cold.
Serves 4-6

CELERY AND BANANA SALAD

The bananas add a special touch to this highly nutritious salad.

2 bananas, peeled and sliced
1 head of celery, finely chopped
2 oz/50 g walnuts, chopped
1 oz/25 g raisins
4 tablespoons double cream
1 teaspoon Dijon mustard
1 teaspoon fresh lemon juice
salt and cayenne pepper

In a large bowl mix the bananas, celery, walnuts and raisins.
In a separate bowl blend the cream with the mustard, lemon juice, salt and cayenne pepper to taste.
Whisk well, then spoon the dressing over the celery and banana mixture. Toss and serve at room temperature.
Serve accompanied by brown bread and butter.
Serves 4-6

CELERY AND GRUYÈRE SALAD

8 stalks of celery
6 oz/175 g Gruyère cheese
2 tablespoons Dijon mustard
½ teaspoon lemon juice
4 fl oz/100 ml double cream
salt and pepper
2 teaspoons fresh chives, finely chopped
crisp lettuce leaves

Cut the celery into 3 inch/8 cm by ½ inch/1 cm sticks. Cut the Gruyère into the same shaped sticks.
In a bowl combine the mustard, lemon juice, salt and pepper to taste. Add the cream and whisk until the dressing is well combined.
Add the celery, cheese and chives and toss the mixture gently. Divide the salad among 4 salad plates lined with crisp lettuce. Serve cold.
Serves 4

CELERY, APPLE AND WALNUT COCKTAIL

8 stalks of celery, cut into ½ inch/1 cm slices
1 Granny Smith apple, cored and peeled
4 fl oz/100 ml sour cream
3 tablespoons redcurrant jelly
6 oz/175 g seedless green grapes, halved
1 tablespoon lemon juice
1 oz/25 g walnuts, finely chopped
crisp lettuce leaves

Cut the apple into ½ inch/1 cm size cubes.
In a bowl combine the sour cream with the redcurrant jelly, whisking vigorously until the mixture is smooth.
Add the apple, celery, grapes and lemon juice and chill the mixture, covered, for at least 1 hour.
Add the walnuts and toss the mixture.
Divide it among 4 chilled salad plates or cocktail glasses lined with lettuce leaves. Serve very cold.
Serves 4

CELERY SURPRISE SOUP

1 head of celery, finely chopped
2 oz/50 g butter
1 oz/25 g cornflour
1¾ pint/1 litre chicken stock
1 (6 fl oz/175 ml) carton single cream
⅛ teaspoon nutmeg, grated
salt and freshly ground black pepper

Place the celery in a saucepan with a little salt and enough water to cover it.
Bring to boil, then simmer until the celery is very tender.
Drain, but reserve half of the water.
In a separate saucepan melt the butter, add the cornflour, stirring constantly.
Slowly add the hot chicken stock and half of the celery water.
Stir constantly. Add the cooked celery and bring the mixture to boil. Stir, then reduce the heat. Simmer, covered, over very low heat for 30 minutes.
Add the pepper, salt and nutmeg. Cook for a further 3-5 minutes.
Cool the mixture, then place it in an electric blender or mixer and blend until very smooth.
Return the mixture to the saucepan and reheat gently.
Add the cream and let it heat thoroughly but without boiling.
Correct the seasoning.
Serve hot.
Serves 4-6

Cheese

The history of cheese-making goes back a long way. Archaeologists claim that cheese was known to the Sumerians (4000BC) as their tablets contain references to it. The early Greeks trained their athletes on cheese, and it also was a main ingredient in the ancient Greek wedding cake. Cheeses were locally produced in most Roman provinces and eaten with bread, or sometimes incorporated in their cookery. In wealthy Roman households there were special ovens for smoking cheese.

In England in the Middle Ages hard cheeses were the staple diet of peasants. They were not yet known by names, but fell into two categories: soft and hard cheese. Hard cheeses, properly made and stored in a dry place, would keep for a long time. In Tudor and Stuart times, cheeses were often coloured with the juice of marigold, spinach or sage.

In France in 1790, a farmer's wife invented by accident the Camembert. A statue has been erected in grateful memory to Mme Harel in the little village of Camembert in France.

There are now over 2,000 different kinds of cheese, 500 in France alone.

We should be grateful to our ancestors who came up with a concentrated food that contains more protein than meat, twice as much calcium as milk and a lot of vitamin A, B, and E.

1 oz/25 g cottage cheese contains 32 calories.
1 oz/25 g cream cheese contains 232 calories.
1 oz /25 g Cheddar cheese contains 117 calories.
1 oz/25 g Gruyère and Stilton contains 134 calories.
1 oz/25 g Parmesan contains 118 calories.

CHEESE PÂTÉ

18 oz/500 g Gruyère cheese, finely grated
1 tablespoon Worcestershire sauce
1 tablespoon vegetable oil
1 teaspoon fresh lemon juice
2 cloves of garlic, crushed
1½ teaspoons powdered English mustard
1 teaspoon paprika
½ teaspoon salt
½ pint/300 ml lager or light beer
1 egg white, stiffly beaten

Combine the cheese, Worcestershire sauce, oil, lemon juice, garlic, mustard, paprika and salt in a mixing bowl.
With a wooden spoon beat all the ingredients together.
Gradually begin to add the beer.
Stir well and fold in the egg white.
Stir again and pour the mixture into an earthenware dish.
Chill for several hours, or overnight.
Serve with brown bread.
Serves 4-8

CREAM CHEESE MOUSSE

1 tin jellied consommé
6 oz/175 g Philadelphia, or any other cream cheese
pinch of curry powder
salt and freshly ground white pepper

Reserve a little of the consommé for garnish.
Pour the rest in a mixing bowl. Add the cream cheese and curry powder.
Beat them together until the mixture is smooth. Season with salt and pepper.
Fill individual ramekin dishes with the mousse. Top each serving with a spoonful of the reserved consommé.
Chill until set.
Serve cold with hot buttered triangles of toast.
Serves 4

CHEDDAR AND PORT MOUSSE

4 tablespoons port
9 oz/250 g Cheddar cheese, diced
2 tablespoons double cream
¼ teaspoon paprika
¼ teaspoon salt
¼ teaspoon onion powder

Place the port, cheese, cream, paprika, salt and onion powder into an electric blender or mixer.
Blend until the mixture is very smooth.
Put the mixture into an earthenware dish, or individual ramekin dishes, and chill for several hours.
Serve cold with thin slices of toast.
Serves 4

BRIE AND GREEN PEPPER MOUSSE

I was served this unusual and excellent starter in a restaurant in Boston, USA.

1 green pepper, seeded and chopped
2 shallots, chopped
1 oz/25 g butter
1 lb/450 g Brie, cut into very small pieces
1 pint/600 ml evaporated milk
¾ pint/450 ml chicken stock
1½ tablespoons powdered gelatine
4 oz/100 g spring onion, chopped

In an electric blender or mixer purée the green pepper with the shallots.
Cook the purée in the butter in a heavy saucepan over moderate heat, stirring, for 5 minutes.
Add the Brie and cook the mixture over low heat until the Brie is melted.
Pour in the milk and the stock, stirring all the time.
Cook the mixture, stirring, for 7 minutes.
Stir in the gelatine and bring the mixture to boil. Cool it a little, then transfer, a small portion at a time, to your electric

blender or mixer and blend until smooth. Transfer each portion to a large bowl.

Fold in the spring onion and turn the mixture into a rinsed bowl.

Chill for at least 6 hours.

Dip the mould into hot water and run a thin knife blade around the edge. Invert a chilled plate over the mould, and turn the mousse onto it. Serve chilled.

Cut the mousse into fairly thin slices with a knife dipped in hot water.

Serves 8-10

CAMEMBERT POTS

1 lb 2 oz/500 g Camembert, not too ripe
1½ pints/900 ml single cream
dash of Worcestershire sauce
salt and freshly ground white pepper
chopped chives
paprika

Peel the rind from the cheese and melt the cheese in a heavy saucepan over low heat.

Slowly stir in the cream, Worcestershire sauce, salt and pepper. Mix well.

Pour the mixture into 6-8 individual little pots and chill for 3-4 hours.

Serve cold. Sprinkle with chives and dust with paprika.

Serves 6-8

POTTED CHEESE

This dish keeps well in the refrigerator for 3-4 days.

8 oz/225 g hard cheese, finely grated
2 oz/50 g butter
1 tablespoon dry sherry
¼ teaspoon powdered English mustard
pinch of nutmeg
salt and freshly ground white pepper

In a heavy saucepan melt the butter. Reserve half.
Add the cheese, sherry, mustard, nutmeg, salt and pepper to the saucepan. Stir well, and when the cheese is melted spoon the mixture into individual small pots.
Brush the tops with the reserved butter.
Chill for several hours. Serve cold with toast or brown bread.
Serves 4

PEARS STUFFED WITH CHEESE

4 pears
3 oz/75 g Gorgonzola, or any other blue cheese
½ oz/25 g butter
¼ pint/150 ml cottage cheese
milk
cayenne pepper to taste

Peel the pears, cut in half and scoop out cores and pips.
In a bowl mash the cheese and butter together, until smooth.
Put a spoonful in the centre of each half pear.
Thin the cottage cheese with a little milk until it is the consistency of thick cream.
Spoon a little over each half pear. Dust with cayenne.
Serve cold.
Serves 4

MOZZARELLA AND TOMATO SALAD

1 lb/450 g big ripe tomatoes, peeled
8 oz/225 g Mozzarella cheese, thinly sliced
1 tablespoon white wine vinegar
salt and freshly ground black pepper
½ teaspoon fresh basil, chopped
3 tablespoons olive oil
black olives

Remove the stalks from the tomatoes and slice them thickly crosswise.
Arrange the tomato and cheese slices in alternate over-lapping layers on a flat serving dish.
Mix the vinegar with the salt and pepper. Add the basil, whisk, and slowly beat in the olive oil.
Spoon the dressing over the tomatoes and cheese.
Garnish with black olives. Serve cold accompanied by hot crusty French bread.
Serves 4

MOZZARELLA ROUNDS WITH SMOKED SALMON

8 slices white bread
8 oz/225 g Mozzarella cheese, cut into 16 thin slices
3 oz/75 g smoked salmon, sliced thin
2-3 oz/50-75 g butter

With a knife trim about 1¾ inch/7 cm-rounds from each slice of bread.
Trim the Mozzarella to the exact size of the rounds.
Heat the butter in a heavy frying-pan and sauté the bread rounds, turning them once, until golden.
With a slotted spoon transfer the rounds to a baking sheet.
Top the rounds with the salmon and the cheese.
Grill about 4 inches/15 cm from the heat for 1-2 minutes, or until the cheese is melted.
Serve very hot.
Serves 4

LIPTAUER CHEESE

This dish will keep in the refrigerator for several days.

¼ pint/150 ml sour cream
18 oz/500 g cream cheese
9 oz/250 g butter, softened
1 small tin anchovies chopped (plus the oil)
2 teaspoons capers, chopped
2 spring onions, finely chopped
½ teaspoon salt
1 tablespoon paprika
2 teaspoons caraway seeds

Put all the ingredients into a bowl and whisk until the mixture is smooth. Serve with hot toast or brown bread.
Serves 6-8

GREEK SALAD WITH FETA CHEESE

This salad, one of the most typical starters of Greece, is very simple to prepare.

1 round lettuce, washed and dried
1 medium cucumber, washed and sliced
1 small green pepper, seeded and sliced
1 lb/450 g Feta cheese
4 tablespoons olive oil
2 tablespoons vinegar
pinch of oregano
12 black Greek olives
salt and freshly ground black pepper

Break the Feta cheese into bite-size pieces.
Tear the lettuce leaves into strips, arrange on a large platter, and sprinkle with some of the olive oil and the vinegar.
Scatter the cucumber, green pepper, olives and Feta cheese over the lettuce.
Pour the remaining oil and vinegar over the top, season with oregano, salt and pepper and serve without tossing it.
Serves 6

GOAT CHEESE WITH ASPIC

8 oz/225 g goat cheese
4 teaspoons powdered gelatine
4 tablespoons tomato juice
1 lb/450 g tomatoes, peeled, chopped and seeded
1 small onion, finely chopped
½ green pepper, finely chopped
2 tablespoons fresh coriander leaves, finely chopped
1 teaspoon lemon juice
4 tablespoons double cream
coriander sprigs for garnish
salt and pepper

In a small heatproof dish combine the tomato juice with 2½ teaspoons of the gelatine and leave to soften for 15 minutes. Set the dish over a larger pan of simmering water and stir the mixture until the gelatine has dissolved.

In a glass bowl combine the tomatoes, onion, green pepper, lemon juice and salt and pepper to taste. Pour this mixture into a rinsed jelly mould. Chill for at least 4 hours, or until it is just set.

In another small heatproof dish combine the remaining gelatine with the cream and let it soften for 15 minutes. Set the dish over a larger pan of simmering water and stir until the gelatine is dissolved.

In another bowl beat the goat cheese until it is fluffy, then beat in the gelatine mixture. Spread the cheese mixture over the aspic and chill the mould, covered, for a further 2 hours, or until it is set.

Dip the mould briefly into hot water, run a thin knife around the edge of the mould, and invert a serving plate over it. Turn the aspic on to the plate. Garnish with sprigs of coriander.

Serve cold.

Serves 4

DEEP-FRIED CAMEMBERT WITH TOMATO SAUCE

8 oz/225 g Camembert, barely ripe
2 oz/50 g flour
1 large egg
1 teaspoon vegetable oil
2 oz/50 g breadcrumbs
vegetable oil for deep frying
1 bunch of parsley, divided into sprigs
½ pint/300 ml tomato sauce, see page 271

Chill the Camembert for 1 hour.
Remove the rind and cut into 8 wedges.
Mix the egg with 1 teaspoon vegetable oil. Coat the Camembert wedges with flour, shaking off the excess, then dip them in the egg mixture, letting excess drip off, and dredge with breadcrumbs, shaking off the excess. Repeat the dredging and dipping procedure, put the well-coated wedges on a plate and chill for 1 hour.
In a deep frying-pan heat the oil. Fry the Camembert wedges, turning, for 2 minutes or until golden.
Transfer the wedges to absorbent kitchen paper to drain, then arrange them on a platter. Keep warm.
Reheat the oil and carefully fry a handful of parsley sprigs, stirring, for 4-6 seconds, or until the oil stops sizzling.
Transfer the parsley with tongs to absorbent kitchen paper to drain. Sprinkle with salt.
Fry the remaining parsley the same way, making sure that the oil is reheated before adding a new batch.
Arrange the Camembert together with the parsley on a platter.
Serve hot with tomato sauce.
Serves 2-4

CHILLED ROQUEFORT AND HAM SOUFFLÉ

3 oz/75 g Roquefort, crumbled
4 oz/100 g cooked ham, chopped
4 fl oz/100 ml cold chicken stock
4 teaspoons powdered gelatine
2 small cloves of garlic, crushed
white pepper to taste
8 fl oz/250 ml double cream, chilled
2 egg whites
pinch of cream of tartar
4 oz/100 g cooked ham, cut into *julienne* strips
mayonnaise, see page 266

Sprinkle the gelatine over the stock and let it stand for 10 minutes in a small bowl.

Set the bowl in a larger bowl of hot water and stir until the gelatine is completely dissolved.

In an electric blender or mixer purée the chopped ham with the Roquefort. Slowly add the stock, then the garlic and white pepper. Blend until smooth.

In a chilled bowl beat the cream until very stiff, then fold it into the cheese and ham mixture.

Beat the egg whites with the cream of tartar until they are very stiff. Fold them gently but thoroughly into the cheese and ham mixture.

Spoon it into a rinsed mould. Cover and chill for at least 4 hours or until it is set.

Dip the mould into hot water for a few seconds. Invert a serving plate over it, then turn the soufflé out onto the plate.

Garnish with strips of *julienne* ham.

Serve with mayonnaise.

Serves 6

FRIED CHEESE CUBES

14 oz/400 g Mozzarella cheese
1-2 eggs, slightly beaten
plain flour for coating
toasted breadcrumbs
vegetable oil for deep frying
basil leaves

Cut the cheese into 1½ inch/3.5 cm cubes. Coat with flour, dip into beaten egg, letting excess drip off, then coat the cheese cubes with breadcrumbs, shaking off excess. Repeat this process of coating with flour, dipping into the egg and coating with breadcrumbs.
Chill the cubes for 1 hour.
In a deep frying-pan heat the oil and fry the cubes, a few at a time, turning until golden brown.
Drain on absorbent kitchen paper.
Arrange the cubes on a warm platter, garnish with basil leaves and serve immediately.
Serves 4

ELEGANT CHEESE SOUP WITH WINE

4 oz/100 g Cheddar cheese, grated
2 oz/50 g butter
1 oz/25 g flour
1 clove of garlic
1¾ pints/1 litre hot milk
4 tablespoons dry white wine
salt to taste
freshly ground white pepper
2 egg yolks
pinch of nutmeg
2 tablespoons single cream

Melt the butter in a double saucepan. Blend in the flour and gradually stir in the hot milk: stir constantly until the mixture becomes smooth. Add the garlic and cook gently for 20 minutes over the simmering water.

Discard the garlic, stir in the Cheddar cheese and the wine.
Season with salt, freshly ground white pepper and nutmeg.
Blend the egg yolks with the cream and add 1 tablespoon of
hot milk to this mixture, then stir it into the soup.
Simmer, stirring constantly, for a further 3 minutes.
Serve immediately.
Serves 4-6

CHEDDAR CHEESE SOUP

*Cheese soup was popular during the First World War. The following
two recipes are up-dated and sophisticated versions.*

2 oz/50 g butter
1 tablespoon onion, finely grated
1 oz/25 g flour
1¾ pints/1 litre warm chicken stock
generous ¾ pint/450 ml milk
8 oz/225 g Cheddar cheese, grated
½ teaspoon white pepper
salt to taste

Melt the butter in a heavy saucepan.
Add the onion and sauté for 5 minutes, or until the onion is
transparent but not browned. Add the flour and stir until the
mixture is smooth. Gradually add the warm broth, stirring
constantly, until boiling point.
Reduce the heat and add the milk, cheese, salt and pepper.
Cook over low heat until the cheese is melted and the soup
begins to bubble.
Correct the seasoning. Serve immediately.
Serves 6

Cucumber

The cucumber originated in north-west India, where it grew in a wild state, and was cultivated by most ancient civilizations.

The Roman emperor Tiberius demanded that cucumber was available every day of the year, and a complicated method for growing it out of season was devised.

Until the sixteenth century cucumbers were little known in England; only towards the end of that century were they grown in greater quantities.

There are a large number of species: white or green, with smooth or rough skin. In the East and Middle East cucumbers are short, plump and sweet, with a lighter skin than the familiar European cucumber.

Cucumbers contain little nutritive value, except for a certain amount of potassium.
4 oz/100 g of cucumber contain 12 calories.

Tip
■ The cucumber contains a rather bitter juice which should be removed by salting for about 30 minutes, then pressing out the juice before preparing and seasoning.

CUCUMBER À LA PROVENÇALE

2 large cucumbers, peeled and seeded
2 large tomatoes, peeled, seeded and chopped
2 cloves of garlic, chopped
1 small fresh red or green hot chilli pepper
2 tablespoons finely chopped parsley
4 tablespoons olive oil
salt and black pepper

Cut the cucumbers into 1½ inches/4 cm by ¾ inch/2 cm pieces.

Wearing rubber gloves, seed and cut the chilli pepper into fine strips.

In a saucepan of boiling water, boil the cucumbers for 3 minutes, drain, then refresh them under running cold water.

In a separate saucepan heat 2 tablespoons of the oil and cook the tomatoes and the garlic, covered, over moderate heat for 10 minutes, stirring occasionally.

In a heavy frying-pan heat the remaining 2 tablespoons of oil and sauté the cucumbers over moderately high heat for 2 minutes.

Add salt and pepper, then add the cucumbers to the tomato mixture.

Stir in the chilli pepper and simmer the mixture for a further 5 minutes. Check the seasoning.

Transfer this mixture to a heated serving dish and sprinkle with the parsley.

Alternatively, let the mixture cool and chill it, covered, in the refrigerator for at least 3 hours.

Serve with crusty hot French bread.

Serves 4

CUCUMBER COCKTAIL WITH YOGHURT DRESSING

1 cucumber, peeled, halved and seeded
2 teaspoons fresh mint, chopped, OR
1 teaspoon dried mint
¼ pint/150 ml natural yoghurt
¼ teaspoon cayenne pepper
1 small clove of garlic, crushed
pinch of sugar
½ teaspoon lemon juice
salt and freshly ground white pepper

Cut the cucumber into ½ inch/1 cm cubes, put them in a bowl and sprinkle them with salt. Cover with a plate and leave, for at least ½ hour, to draw out the juices.
Drain the diced cucumber and pat dry.
In a separate bowl mix the yoghurt with the mint, garlic, cayenne, sugar, lemon juice, salt and pepper. Blend well and pour over the cucumber. Toss the cucumber in the yoghurt dressing. Garnish with a little chopped mint.
Serve chilled in glasses or bowls.
Serves 4

CUCUMBERS À LA GRÈCQUE

1 large cucumber, peeled, halved and seeded
½ pint/300 ml water
3 tablespoons olive oil
1 (2¼ oz/63 g) tin tomato paste
3 teaspoons onion, finely grated
1 small clove of garlic, crushed
1 sprig of parsley
¼ teaspoon dried thyme
pinch of dried fennel
1 bay leaf
6 coriander seeds
6 white peppercorns
salt to taste
fresh parsley, chopped

Cut the cucumber into ½ inch/1 cm pieces.
In a heavy saucepan combine all ingredients, except the cucumber.
Bring to boil, then add the cucumber.
Simmer, stirring occasionally, for 15 minutes.
With a slotted spoon remove the cucumber from the liquid.
Place the drained cucumber in a bowl.
Strain the liquid through a colander over the cucumber.
Chill for several hours.
Serve in individual glasses or bowls. Sprinkle with parsley.
Serve chilled.
Serves 4

GERMAN CUCUMBER SALAD

2 cucumbers
1 teaspoon coarse salt
4 tablespoons tarragon vinegar
4 tablespoons water
1 teaspoon sugar
¼-½ teaspoon white pepper

With a fork score the cucumbers lengthwise and slice them, very thinly, crosswise.
Put the sliced cucumbers into a bowl and sprinkle with salt.
Cover and leave for 30 minutes.
In a small enamel or stainless steel saucepan combine the vinegar, water, sugar and pepper.
Bring the liquid to boil and stir until the sugar is completely dissolved.
Set aside.
Drain the cucumbers in a colander, then rinse under running cold water and pat them dry.
In a glass bowl mix the cucumber slices with the dressing.
Toss well, correct the seasoning and serve on chilled plates.
Serves 4-6

MULLED CUCUMBER BAKED IN CREAM

3 lb/1.4 kg cucumbers, peeled, seeded and cut
into thick match-sticks
1 medium onion, finely chopped
2 oz/50 g butter
½ teaspoon salt
6 coriander seeds
coarsely ground white pepper
8 fl oz/225 ml dry white wine
1 tablespoon white wine vinegar
2 teaspoons lemon rind, grated
1 tablespoon fresh parsley, chopped
1½ tablespoons fresh thyme, finely chopped, OR
½ teaspoon dried thyme
cayenne pepper to taste
8 fl oz/225 ml sour cream
3 tablespoons double cream

In a heavy saucepan, cook the onion in most of the butter over moderate heat, stirring, until transparent. Add the cucumber, salt, coriander and pepper to taste. Cook, stirring occasionally, for 5 minutes. Add the wine, vinegar, lemon rind, parsley, thyme and cayenne to taste. Simmer for 5 minutes, stirring from time to time.

Strain the liquid from the saucepan, remove the coriander seeds and let the liquid cool.

Stir in 6 fl oz/150 ml of the sour cream. Gently reheat the mixture, stirring, until hot. Don't let it boil, or it will curdle.

In a separate bowl combine the remaining sour cream and the double cream.

Divide the cucumber mixture between 6 ramekins. Top each serving with a rounded tablespoon of the mixed creams and arrange the ramekins on a baking sheet.

Bake in a preheated oven (425°F/220°C/Gas Mark 7) for 5 minutes, or until heated through.

Serve immediately.

Serves 6

CUCUMBER MOUSSE

The ideal summer starter!

2 large cucumbers, peeled, seeded and chopped
2 oz/50 g powdered gelatine
½ pint/300 ml chicken stock
1 tablespoon fresh lemon juice
12 oz/350 g cream cheese
4 tablespoons mayonnaise, see page 266
¼ teaspoon curry powder
salt and freshly ground white pepper

Purée the cucumbers in an electric blender or mixer.
Soften the gelatine in a little stock.
Blend the remaining stock with the lemon juice. Add it to the gelatine and dissolve over gentle heat, stirring constantly.
In a bowl beat the cream cheese until soft; gradually add the mayonnaise and the warm gelatine mixture. Whisk until smooth. Blend in the cucumber purée, curry powder, salt and pepper. Rinse a mould, pour in the mousse and chill in the refrigerator for several hours, or until firm.
To turn it out: dip the mould briefly into hot water, then run a thin knife blade round the edge of the mousse, invert a chilled serving plate over the top, and turn the dish and the plate over together. Give a sharp shake to dislodge the mousse.
Serve chilled.
Serves 8

CUCUMBER AND YOGHURT MOUSSE

1 large cucumber, peeled and seeded
4 oz/100 g cream cheese
juice of 1 lemon
2 tablespoons double cream
¼ pint/150 ml natural yoghurt
salt and freshly ground white pepper
grated nutmeg
dash of tabasco sauce
¼ teaspoon dried dill weed
¼ pint/150 ml chicken stock
½ oz/25 g powdered gelatine

Grate the cucumber, but reserve a few narrow strips for garnish.
In a bowl beat together the cream cheese, lemon juice, cream and yoghurt. Fold in the grated cucumber and season with salt and pepper, grated nutmeg, tabasco and dill.
Put the stock in a small saucepan and sprinkle in the gelatine. Leave it for a few minutes until it looks syrupy, then warm it over gentle heat, stirring, until it is completely dissolved.
Stir it briskly into the cucumber mixture. Pour the cucumber mixture into a rinsed mould, and chill in the refrigerator for several hours, or until set.
To turn it out: dip the mould briefly into hot water, then run a thin knife blade around the edge of the mould, invert a chilled plate over the top, and turn the plate and the mould over together. Give a sharp shake to dislodge the mousse.
Use the remaining cucumber strips for garnish. Serve chilled.
Serves 4

COLD CUCUMBER SOUP

1 cucumber, peeled, seeded and diced
2½ pints/1.5 litre chicken stock
1 (5 fl oz/142 ml) carton sour cream
¼ teaspoon cayenne pepper
salt and freshly ground white pepper

¾ teaspoon lemon rind, finely grated
fresh chives, or green spring onion tops,
finely chopped

Cook the cucumber in the stock until soft.
Put the mixture into an electric blender or mixer and blend until smooth. Pour into a bowl and cool.
Add the sour cream, cayenne, salt and pepper. Stir well, then add the lemon rind and stir again.
Chill, covered, in the refrigerator for several hours.
Just before serving correct the seasoning.
Serve chilled in chilled soup bowls. Sprinkle with chives or spring onion tops.
Serves 4-6

CREAM OF CUCUMBER SOUP

1 lb/450 g cucumber, diced, seeded but unpeeled
1 small leek (white part only) chopped
4 oz/100 g raw potatoes, diced
1 tablespoon parsley, finely chopped
1 pint/600 ml chicken stock
¼ teaspoon powdered English mustard
salt to taste
freshly ground white pepper
1 (5 fl oz/142 ml) carton double cream
fresh chives or spring onion tops, finely chopped

In a heavy saucepan combine the chicken stock, cucumber, leek, potatoes, parsley, mustard powder, salt and pepper.
Bring to boil skim the surface, reduce the heat and simmer, covered, until all the vegetables are tender.
Put the mixture in an electric blender or mixer and blend until very smooth.
Return the mixture to the saucepan and reheat very gently.
Add the cream and heat through, without boiling or the soup will curdle. Correct the seasoning.
Serve hot in warm soup bowls. Sprinkle each portion with chopped chives.
Serves 4

Egg

Long before the domestication of the hen, wild eggs were among the first foods of primitive men.

For a long time the egg was seen as a symbol of fertility and it was believed that the universe was born from a great Mother egg. German and Slav peasants used to smear their ploughs with a mixture of egg, flour and bread on the Thursday before Easter to ensure a good harvest.

The egg was an important ingredient in Roman cookery: it was used as a thickening and binding agent for other food. Later, from the Greeks, the Romans borrowed the idea of combining egg with milk to form a custard mixture.

In England the earliest type of omelette was known as 'herbolace' in the late fourteenth century. It was a mixture of eggs and shredded herbs baked in a buttered dish. In the Middle Ages new-laid eggs were eaten roasted with salt and sugar. By the sixteenth century the boiling of eggs in their shells became common practice, because they were more digestible than roasted eggs.

Buttered eggs were the forerunners of scrambled eggs and appeared in England in the seventeenth century.

Raw and soft-boiled eggs are easily digestible. Eggs have the most perfect protein components of any food, and the egg yolk contains lecithin which aids fat assimilation.

Eggs contain iron and vitamins A, B, D, and E.

1 boiled egg contains, according to size, between 87-92 calories.
1 raw egg yolk contains between 69-79 calories.
1 raw egg white contains between 18-20 calories.

Tips
■ In order to peel hard-boiled eggs properly, it is necessary to plunge them into cold water as soon as they are cooked.
■ Add a pinch of salt to egg whites before beating them.
■ If you make a sauce with egg yolks, do not let it boil, or the mixture will be full of little yellow threads.
■ Egg whites have to be used up quickly. Once they are separated from the yolk, they must be used the same day.
■ To boil a cracked egg, add vinegar and salt to the water and the crack will be sealed.
■ When frying eggs, add a little flour to the pan to prevent sticking.

OEUFS EN GELÉE

This easy starter can be prepared well in advance.
The tarragon must be fresh.

4 eggs
1 tin consommé
2 sprigs of fresh tarragon
freshly ground white pepper
few drops of lemon juice

Pour the consommé into a pan with 2 sprigs of tarragon, a few drops of lemon juice and freshly ground white pepper.
Boil for 1 minute, then leave to cool, removing one sprig.
Keep the second, blanched one, for garnish.
Boil the egg for 5 minutes. The egg yolk must be slightly runny. Shell the eggs under cold water and put each egg into a separate ramekin dish. Pour the consommé over it.
Garnish with blanched tarragon leaves.
Chill in the refrigerator for several hours or until set.
Serve cold.
Serves 4

EGGS STUFFED WITH ANCHOVY

6 eggs, hard-boiled and shelled
3 oz/75 g toasted breadcrumbs
4 tablespoons milk
1 small tin anchovies, drained
2 tomatoes, sliced

Soak the breadcrumbs in milk. Finely chop the anchovy fillets.
Cut the eggs lengthwise and remove the yolks.
Drain the breadcrumbs and mix them with the anchovy fillets and the egg yolks. Mix it well and fill the hollow of the eggs with this mixture.
Garnish with sliced tomatoes.
Serve cold.
Serves 6

EGG MAYONNAISE

4 eggs, hard-boiled
mayonnaise, see page 266
shredded lettuce leaves
paprika

Cut the eggs lengthwise and serve them on a bed of shredded lettuce. Spoon mayonnaise over them. Dust with paprika. Serve cold.
Serves 4

EGGS JAQUELINE

4 eggs, hard-boiled and shelled
2 oz/50 g butter
½ teaspoon paprika
6 oz/175 g cooked prawns, shelled
12 oz/350 g asparagus, cooked, see page 27
½ pint/300 ml béchamel sauce, see page 270
2 tablespoons Parmesan, grated
salt and pepper to taste

Cut the eggs lengthwise, remove yolks, and place the whites in a bowl of water if they are not to be used immediately.
Finely chop a third of the prawns.
In a bowl combine the butter, egg yolks and paprika. Blend well, then add the chopped prawns. Season to taste.
Place the asparagus in a buttered ovenproof dish, or divide it between 4 individual ovenproof dishes. Fill the hollow of the egg whites with the prawn mixture and place them on the asparagus. Scatter the remaining whole prawns over the top, coat with béchamel sauce and sprinkle with Parmesan cheese.
Bake in a preheated oven (300°F/150°C/Gas Mark 2) for 15 minutes, or until it is golden brown.
Serve hot.
Serves 4

BRANDIED STUFFED EGGS

6 eggs, hard-boiled and shelled
6 black olives, pitted and chopped
3 tablespoons capers
4 teaspoons flaked tuna
2 tablespoons brandy
½ teaspoon Dijon mustard
pinch of allspice
olive oil
3 tomatoes, peeled and sliced
1 lb/450 g French green beans, cooked
French dressing, see page 265
freshly ground black pepper

Cut each egg in half lengthwise and remove the yolk.
In a bowl mash the yolks with a fork, add the olives, capers, tuna, mustard, allspice, brandy and black pepper. Add a little olive oil and blend it into a smooth paste. Correct the seasoning. Fill the hollow of each egg white with this mixture.
In a separate bowl mix the sliced tomatoes with the beans.
Spoon over some French dressing to taste. Toss and correct the seasoning.
Place the stuffed eggs surrounded by the beans and tomatoes on a chilled platter.
Serve very cold.
Serves 6

EGGS MIMOSA

8 eggs, hard-boiled and shelled
1 teaspoon Dijon mustard
¼ pint/150 ml mayonnaise, see page 266
2 tablespoons fresh *fines herbes* (chopped chervil,
tarragon and parsley) OR
1 tablespoon dried *fines herbes*
salt and pepper
crisp lettuce leaves
paprika

Cut the eggs in half lengthwise. Remove the yolks and in a bowl, mash 3 yolks.

In a separate bowl mix the mustard with the mayonnaise. Add the mashed yolks and the *fines herbes*. Season with salt and pepper, and blend until the mixture is smooth.

Pile the mixture into the hollows of the egg whites and place them on a serving platter lined with crisp lettuce leaves.

Chop the remaining egg yolks very finely and sprinkle them over the eggs. Dust with paprika.

Serves 8

EGG AND PRAWN MOUSSE

6 eggs, hard-boiled and shelled
7 oz/200 g prawns, cooked and shelled
1 teaspoon anchovy essence
2 tablespoons medium dry sherry
1 large tin consommé
¼ pint/150 ml double cream, whipped
salt and pepper

Separate the hard-boiled egg yolks from the whites. Chop the whites and set aside.

Chop the prawns but leave a few whole for garnish.

In a bowl mash the yolks with a fork. Add the anchovy essence, sherry, chopped egg whites and prawns. Mix well, then whisk in three-quarters of the consommé. Whisk again and fold in the whipped cream. Season with salt and pepper and beat the mousse until frothy.

Pour the mousse into a dish and let it set in the refrigerator.

Garnish the top with the remaining whole prawns. Melt the rest of the consommé and pour it over the top to set the garnish.

Chill, covered, for several hours, or overnight.

Serves 4-6

EGG CUSTARDS WITH TOMATO SAUCE

4 eggs
salt and freshly ground white pepper
1 pint/600 ml milk
2 oz/50 g Gruyère cheese, grated
tomato sauce, see page 271

In a large bowl beat the eggs, adding a pinch of salt.
Put the milk into a saucepan, add salt and pepper, and bring to boiling point.
Remove the milk from the heat and pour it in a slow stream over the eggs, beating them vigorously.
Beat in the cheese, and continue beating until the cheese is melted.
Butter 6 large ramekins and pour in the egg mixture.
Stand the dishes in a large, shallow pan of simmering water and cook for 20 minutes, or until the eggs are set in the centre. Serve hot with hot tomato sauce.
Serves 4

POACHED EGG SALAD

2 tablespoons cider- or white wine vinegar
6 eggs
6 slices tomato, peeled, 1 inch/2.5 cm thick
crisp lettuce leaves, shredded
salt and pepper
½ teaspoon fresh basil, chopped, OR
pinch of dried basil
½ pint/300 ml mayonnaise, see page 266
3 tablespoons tomato ketchup
few drops tabasco sauce
2 tablespoons fresh chives (or spring onion tops), chopped
2 tablespoons fresh parsley, chopped

Fill a wide shallow saucepan with water and add the vinegar. Bring to boil, then reduce the heat so that the liquid barely simmers.

Break the eggs, one at a time, into a saucer and slide them into the liquid. As each egg drops in, push the egg white immediately towards the yolk. Simmer the eggs for 3 minutes, then transfer them with a slotted spoon to a bowl of cold water.

Arrange each tomato slice on a nest of shredded lettuce. Sprinkle with salt and pepper and a little basil. Put a well trimmed egg on top.

Mix the mayonnaise with the ketchup, tabasco, the remaining basil, chives and parsley.

Blend well and spoon this mixture over the eggs.

Serve very cold.

Serves 6

EGGS FLAMENCO

2 oz/50 g butter
1 tablespoon oil
2 medium onions, sliced
1 clove of garlic, crushed
2 red peppers, seeded and sliced
1 (8 oz/225 g) tin tomatoes
1 teaspoon Worcestershire sauce
dash of tabasco sauce
4 eggs
salt and fresh ground black pepper

Fry the onions and the garlic in the butter and oil until the onions are transparent. Add the peppers and continue to cook for 2-3 minutes. Pour in the tomatoes with their juice, Worcestershire sauce, tabasco, salt and pepper to taste.

Bring to boil, then reduce the heat and simmer until all ingredients are tender, but not mushy, and the liquid has almost evaporated.

Divide the mixture between 4 small ovenproof dishes. Make a hollow in the centres and break 1 egg into each dish.

Bake in a preheated oven at 425°F/220°C/Gas Mark 7 for 10 minutes, or until the eggs are just set.

Serve immediately.

Serves 4

PEPPERED EGGS

2 large green peppers, halved and seeded
8 oz/250 g mushrooms, sliced
1 tablespoon olive oil
4 eggs
2 oz/50 g Cheddar cheese, grated
salt and freshly ground black pepper

Cook the peppers in boiling water for 6 minutes.
Strain and place in an ovenproof dish.
In a heavy saucepan sauté the mushrooms gently in the olive oil for 2-3 minutes. With a slotted spoon drain them on absorbent kitchen paper.
Divide the mushrooms among the 4 pepper halves.
Break an egg on top of the mushrooms in each pepper.
Season with salt and pepper and sprinkle with grated cheese.
Bake for 15 minutes in a moderate oven at 375°F/190°C/Gas Mark 5.
Serve immediately.
Serves 4

EGGS BENEDICT

*I first learned of this recipe in New York from my friend
Luce Neilson who served it for 'brunch'. Although it's a fairly rich
dish, it makes a very tempting starter.*

8 fl oz/25 ml hollandaise sauce, see page 270
1 pint/600 ml water
1 tablespoon cider- or white wine vinegar
6 eggs
6 slices cooked ham, cut fairly thick
2 tablespoons sherry
6 slices white bread, cut into 3 inch/7.5 cm rounds
½ oz/15 g butter
salt

Prepare the hollandaise sauce and keep it warm.
To poach the eggs:
In a large shallow saucepan combine the water and the

vinegar. Bring to boil, then reduce to simmering.

Break the eggs, one at a time, into a saucer and slide them into the liquid. As each egg drops in, push the white immediately towards the yolk. Simmer for 3 minutes, or until set, without the eggs being hard. Lift each egg out separately, letting it drain over the pan. Keep the eggs warm. Preheat the oven to 250°F/120°C/Gas Mark 1.

Cut the ham into rounds so that they are the same size as the bread-rounds. Place the ham in an ovenproof dish, pour over the sherry and cover tightly with foil. Place in the oven to warm.

Toast the bread-rounds and butter them. Place a slice of drained ham on each round, then place a poached and thoroughly drained egg on each slice of ham.

Spoon the hollandaise sauce over the eggs and serve without delay.

Serves 6

TARRAGON BAKED EGGS

4 eggs
½ oz/15 g butter
4 tablespoons double cream
12 fresh tarragon leaves
salt and coarsely ground white pepper

Grease 4 ramekin dishes with the butter.

Break an egg into each dish and pour a tablespoon of cream over each of them. Season with salt and pepper and place 3 tarragon leaves on each dish.

Stand the ramekins in a roasting tin two-thirds full of hot water. Bake in a hot, preheated oven (425°F/220°C/Gas Mark 7) for 12 minutes, or until the whites are just set and the yolks still runny.

Serve immediately.

Serves 4

POACHED EGGS HOLLANDAISE IN POTATO SHELLS

4 large baking potatoes
2 stalks celery, finely chopped
1 small onion, finely chopped
1 oz/25 g butter
3 oz/75 g prawns, cooked and peeled
4 tablespoons dry white wine
¼ teaspoon Worcestershire sauce
salt and pepper
8 large eggs
2 tablespoons cider- or white wine vinegar
½ pint/300 ml hollandaise sauce, see page 270
1 oz/25 g Parmesan cheese, grated

Bake the potatoes in a preheated oven (375°F/190°C/Gas Mark 5) for 1 hour, or until they are tender. Let them cool, halve them and scoop out the pulp, leaving a ¼ inch/0.5 cm shell. Discard the pulp, or reserve it for another use.

Simmer the celery and chopped onion in the butter until they are softened. Add the prawns and cook, stirring all the time, for 2 minutes. Add the white wine, Worcestershire sauce, salt and pepper. Mix, heat through and keep warm.

To poach the eggs

In a large shallow saucepan combine about 1 pint/600 ml of water with the vinegar and a pinch of salt. Bring to boil, then reduce the liquid to simmering. Break 1 egg at a time into a saucer and slide the egg into the simmering liquid. As each egg drops in, push the egg white gently towards the yolk with the help of a slotted spoon. Let the eggs simmer for about 3 minutes. Lift each egg out separately with a slotted spoon, letting it drain over the pan, then transfer them to a bowl of cold water.

Divide the celery and prawn mixture among the potato shells. Top each shell with a well-drained poached egg. Arrange the potatoes in an ovenproof dish. Spoon the hollandaise sauce over it and sprinkle with Parmesan.

Put the dish under the hot grill until the cheese is golden.

Serve hot.

Serves 8

EGG CROQUETTES

4 eggs, hard-boiled, shelled and chopped
1 egg
½ pint/300 ml thick béchamel sauce, see page 270
1 large onion, chopped
4 slices bacon, diced
1 oz/25 g butter
1 tablespoon parsley, finely chopped
breadcrumbs
salt and freshly ground white pepper
oil for frying
juice of half a lemon

Sauté the onion and the bacon in the butter until the onion is golden.

In a large bowl combine the hard-boiled eggs, onion, bacon, parsley, cold béchamel sauce and salt and pepper. Mix well, then form the mixture into small oval shapes.

In a separate bowl beat the remaining egg. Have the breadcrumbs ready on a plate.

Dip the croquettes first in the egg mixture, letting excess drip off, then dredge with breadcrumbs, shaking off excess. Put the well coated croquettes on a plate and chill for 1 hour.

In a heavy frying-pan fry the croquettes until golden, turning from time to time. Drain on absorbent kitchen paper, then place them on a serving platter, or individual small plates.

Serve hot, sprinkled with lemon juice.

Serves 4

EGGS FLORENTINE

4 eggs
2 lb/900 g fresh or frozen spinach
1 tablespoon olive oil
3-4 tablespoons Parmesan cheese, grated
butter
¼ pint/150 ml béchamel sauce, see page 270
salt and pepper

If the spinach is frozen, cook while still frozen without water and according to directions on the packet.

To cook fresh spinach

Wash the spinach discarding the stalks. In a large saucepan heat the olive oil, add the spinach leaves, cover and cook for about 5 minues. Season with salt and pepper, cook for another few minutes, stirring, so that all the leaves are coated with oil. Drain the spinach and refresh it under running cold water.

Lightly butter an ovenproof dish. Arrange the hot spinach in it, but pile it in a little higher at the edges than in the middle.

Press 4 hollows into the spinach with the back of a spoon.

Pour a little melted butter into each hollow. Carefully break one egg into each hollow, sprinkle with Parmesan and spoon a little béchamel sauce over each egg.

Bake in the oven for 10-15 minutes at 350°F/180°C/Gas Mark 4.

Serve hot.

Serves 4

Rich *Brown Bean Soup*, left (see page 60), *Elegant Cheese Soup with Wine,* top
(see page 90) and, right, *Quick Iced Asparagus Soup* (see page 32).

Mussels in Dilled Cucumber Sauce (see page 148).

Simple and inexpensive, above left, *Marinated Mushrooms* (see page 180) and
Marinated Bean Salad (see page 58).

Based on the classic Salad Niçoise, *Tuna Salad Niçoise*, below left, can be prepared
easily for any number of people (see page 128).

Two colourful starters: *Apples Stuffed with Crabmeat* (see page 163) and *Lemons Stuffed with Sardine Mousse* (see page 162).

TO MAKE AN OMELETTE

An omelette is easy to make, and just as easy to spoil. But a little practice and a few special tips should produce the perfect omelette.

1 Always use a spotlessly clean, heavy iron pan.
2 Use just enough butter in the pan to keep the omelette from sticking. Never too much, or the omelette will be greasy and indigestible.
3 Beat the eggs just before seasoning and cooking. Do not beat them too much if you want a soft omelette.
4 As soon as the omelette is cooked slide a few small bits of butter under it to help loosen it from the pan and to give it a shiny appearance.

BASIC OMELETTE FOR FOUR SERVINGS

8 eggs
1 teaspoon salt
pinch of pepper
1½ oz/40 g butter

In a bowl beat the eggs and season them.
Heat the pan over medium heat for about 1-2 minutes.
Add the butter, which should froth immediately, swirl it round the pan and pour in the eggs.
Reduce the heat. The eggs will coagulate on the bottom.
With a wooden spatula lift the edge, first in one place, then in another, tilting the pan slightly to let the liquid egg run under. It should stay quite moist on the top.
When the omelette has browned slightly on the bottom, slide a few bits of butter under it to help loosen it from the pan.
Fold it in two with a spatula and slide it to a warm platter.
Serve immediately.

OMELETTE FINES HERBES

8 eggs
4 tablespoons fresh *fines herbes*, chopped
(chervil, parsley and tarragon), OR
2 tablespoons dried *fines herbes*
salt and pepper

Beat the *fines herbes*, the salt and pepper into the eggs.
Follow the basic omelette instructions.
Serves 4

TOMATO OMELETTE

3-4 tomatoes, peeled, seeded and chopped
2½ tablespoons vegetable oil
8 eggs
1½ oz/40 g butter
salt and pepper

In a heavy saucepan sauté the tomatoes in the oil for 15
minutes.
Drain all the oil off and season tomatoes with salt and
pepper. Set aside and keep warm.
Follow the basic omelette instructions, but do not fold the
omelette. Slide it unfolded onto a warmed serving dish, fill it
with the cooked tomatoes, then fold it in two.
Garnish with little mounds of tomato on either side of the
plate.
Serve immediately.
Serves 4

MUSHROOM OMELETTE

8 oz/225 g button mushrooms, coarsely chopped
1½ oz/40 g butter
1 oz/25 g flour
¼ pint/150 ml milk
6 eggs
2 oz/50 g butter
salt and pepper
1½ oz/40 g butter for the omelette

In a heavy pan melt 1½ oz/40 g butter and sauté the mushrooms until they are soft.

In a separate saucepan melt 2 oz/50 g butter over medium heat until it is foaming. Add the flour and whisk it into a thick paste. Remove the pan from the heat and add the milk in a steady stream, stirring constantly. Return the pan to a low heat and whisk until the sauce is smooth. Season, then add the mushroom juices together with the mushrooms. Stir well, then simmer for a further 3-4 minutes, stirring frequently.

Follow the **basic omelette** instructions, but before folding the omelette, pour half of the mushroom sauce across the middle of it. Fold it over and slide it onto a warmed serving platter before pouring the remaining sauce on top.

Serve immediately.

Serves 6

TO MAKE A SOUFFLÉ

The basic soufflé for starters is a mixture of flour, butter,
milk and eggs, to which different flavoured ingredients are added.
A savoury soufflé makes a perfect beginning to any meal.
And observing the basic rules, it is an easy dish to prepare.

1 The egg yolks must be beaten one by one into the hot sauce after the pan is removed from the heat, otherwise they will curdle.
2 The egg whites must be beaten stiff but not too dry.
3 When separating the eggs, make sure that there is no speck of yolk left in the white, or you will not be able to beat your whites stiff.
4 And finally, the soufflé has to be eaten at once. Serve it, without any delay, straight from the oven.

CHEESE SOUFFLÉ

6 eggs, separated
2 oz/50 g Gruyère cheese, finely grated
2 oz/50 g Parmesan cheese, finely grated

for the sauce
2 oz/50 g butter
2 oz/50 g flour
½ pint/300 ml milk
salt and pepper
pinch of nutmeg

Heat the oven to moderately hot, 400°F/200°C/Gas Mark 6.
Brush a 7¼ inch/18 cm soufflé dish with melted butter.
In a saucepan melt the butter over medium heat, add the flour and whisk constantly.
Remove the saucepan from the heat and gradually add the milk, whisking all the time. Return the saucepan to a low heat, whisking, until the sauce begins to thicken. Season with salt and pepper and add the nutmeg.
Take the saucepan off the heat and beat in the egg yolks, one at a time; then sprinkle in the two cheeses and stir vigorously until they are melted. Leave it to cool.

Beat the whites stiff 35 minutes before serving.

Very gently, with a wooden spatula, fold a third of the egg white into the sauce. Do not stir. Add the rest of the egg white the same way: gently fold, but do not beat or stir.

Pour the mixture into the soufflé dish until it is three-quarters full.

Place it in the oven immediately and cook for 20 minutes.

Increase the heat to 450°F/230°C/Gas Mark 8 and cook for a further 10 minutes. Serve at once.

Serves 6

ONION SOUFFLÉ

2 lb/900 g onions, finely sliced
4 oz/100 g butter
6 eggs, separated

for the sauce
2 oz/50 g butter
2 oz/50 g flour
½ pint/300 ml milk
pinch of hot paprika
pinch of nutmeg
salt and pepper
2 tablespoons double cream

Heat the oven to 400°F/200°C/Gas Mark 6.

Blanch the onions in boiling water for a few minutes, remove them with a slotted spoon and drain them well. In a large heavy pan, melt 2 oz/50 g of the butter and sauté the onions until they are transparent. In a separate saucepan melt the butter over medium heat, add the flour and whisk constantly. Remove the saucepan from the heat and gradually add the milk, whisking all the time. Return to a low heat, whisking, until the sauce begins to thicken.

Add the sauce to the onions then add salt and pepper, nutmeg and paprika. Cook for 10 minutes, stirring constantly, until the sauce is very thick.

Place the mixture into an electric blender or mixer and blend it to a smooth paste.

Beat in the double cream and the remaining butter, cut into small pieces. Beat in the egg yolks, one at a time. Cool the mixture and fold in the stiffly beaten egg whites. Three-quarters fill a soufflé dish and cook for 20 minutes in the oven, then increase the oven temperature to 450°F/230°C/Gas Mark 8 and cook for a further ten minutes.
Serve at once.
Serves 6

HAM SOUFFLÉ

6 eggs, separated
5 oz/150 g lean cooked ham, finely chopped

for the sauce
2 oz/50 g flour
2 oz/50 g butter
½ pint/300 ml milk
salt and pepper
pinch of nutmeg

Heat the oven to 350°F/180°C/Gas Mark 4.
Brush a 7¼ inch/18 cm diameter soufflé dish with melted butter. In a saucepan melt the butter over medium heat, add the flour and whisk constantly.
Remove the saucepan from the heat and gradually add the milk, whisking all the time. Return the saucepan to a low heat, whisking until the sauce begins to thicken.
Season, but not too much salt because the ham itself is salty, and add the nutmeg.
Take the saucepan off the heat and beat in the egg yolks, one at a time. Add the ham, stir and let the sauce cool.
Beat the egg whites stiff 35 minutes before serving.
Very gently, with a wooden spatula, fold a third of the egg white into the sauce. Add the rest of the white the same way: gently fold, but do not beat or stir.
Pour the mixture into the buttered soufflé dish and bake for 10 minutes; then increase heat to 450°F/230°C/Gas mark 8. Cook for a further 20 minutes. Serve at once.
Serves 6

Fish and Shellfish

For centuries fish has formed an important part in the diet of men.

The early Romans had an amazing variety of ways of preparing fish. Rich Romans used a seasoning called 'Liquamen' or 'Garum', which was a sauce made from sprats, anchovies, mackerels, or even white fish and shellfish; whatever the ingredient, 'Liquamen' was usually a golden, clear liquid that kept well in a bottle. It was so popular that it was factory produced. The nearest thing to that fermented fish sauce is still found in South-East Asia today.

In Britain, during the first few centuries after the end of the Roman rule, shellfish lost their appeal as a delicacy, and only in the eighth century did it regain its popularity. In medieval times, fish was eaten on Fridays, on fast days and during Lent when meat was forbidden. By the Elizabethan times, religious observance of fast days was declining, but as meat was still in short supply, the queen passed a law enforcing three meatless days per week.

It is not surprising that Elizabethan cooks were far more adventurous in preparing fish than we are today, for fish played an important part in their daily diet. Fish was also considered to be beneficial for the brain, but this could have been based on a nursery tale to persuade disobedient children to eat up!

All oily fish, such as herring, mackerel, sardines, salmon, tuna and eel contain phosphorus, calcium and vitamins A, B and D. Oily fish contain 45-100 calories per oz/25 g, depending on the preparation of the fish.

White fish, like plaice, sole, turbot, halibut, cod, carp, brill etc, contain phosphorus, iodine and vitamin B. The calorie content is considerably lower, between 25-50 calories per oz/25 g.

Shellfish contain phosphorus, calcium, iodine, iron and vitamin B. The calorie content varies between 14-33 calories per oz/25 g.

SMOKED SALMON WITH CAPERS

8 slices smoked salmon
2-3 teaspoons capers, drained
freshly ground black pepper
lemon wedges
buttered slices of thinly cut brown bread

Divide the salmon slices between 4 plates.
Sprinkle each serving with capers and freshly ground black pepper.
Garnish with lemon wedges.
Serve with buttered brown bread.
Serves 4

SMOKED SALMON ROLLS

4 large slices smoked salmon
2 cartons potted shrimps
juice of 1 lemon
cayenne pepper
4 lemon wedges
watercress

Empty the cartons of potted shrimps into a bowl.
Sprinkle with plenty of lemon juice and dust with cayenne.
Mix well.
Put a quarter of the shrimps on each slice of salmon and roll up the slice.
Garnish with watercress and serve with buttered brown bread and wedges of lemon.
Serves 4

SMOKED SALMON WITH HEARTS OF PALM

8 slices of smoked salmon
1 small tin of hearts of palm, drained
1 tablespoon white wine vinegar
2 tablespoons white wine
2 tablespoons vegetable oil
fresh parsley, dill or fennel for garnish

for the sauce
4 tablespoons mayonnaise, see page 266
6 drops tabasco sauce
1 teaspoon paprika
1 tablespoon red pepper, finely chopped
1 tablespoon green pepper, finely chopped
1 tablespoon fresh chives, finely chopped
½ teaspoon sugar
1 tablespoon beetroot, cooked, peeled and chopped
2 tablespoons sour cream

Drain the hearts of palm. Mix the vinegar with the wine and oil. Pour it over the hearts of palm and marinate, covered, in the refrigerator for 45 minutes.

With a slotted spoon remove the hearts of palm from the marinade, drain and wrap each in a slice of smoked salmon.

Arrange the salmon rolls on a flat dish and sprinkle with chopped parsley, dill or fennel.

In a bowl mix all the ingredients for the sauce, blend well and serve in a sauce-boat.

Serves 4

HERB-MARINATED SALMON

*I was served this magnificent starter in a restaurant in Bergen
in Norway. It is expensive but worth every mouthful.*

1½ lb/675 g whole salmon fillet
1 large onion, sliced thinly
1 tablespoon sugar
1 tablespoon salt
3½ oz/100 g fresh dill, chopped
3½ oz/100 g fresh tarragon, chopped
8 juniper berries, crushed
freshly ground white pepper
5 tablespoons lemon juice
4 tablespoons dry vermouth
¾ pint/450 ml dry white wine
crisp lettuce leaves
green mayonnaise, see page 268

Mix the sugar with the salt and rub it into the salmon.

Take a glass dish large enough to hold the salmon. In it
spread the onion, sprinkled with dill, tarragon, the crushed
juniper berries and pepper. Pour in the lemon juice,
vermouth and wine.

Arrange the salmon, skin side up, on this mixture. Cover the
salmon with cling film and weigh it down with a 5 lb weight.

Let the salmon marinate in the refrigerator for 3 days,
turning it each day.

Transfer it to a cutting board and scrape off the herb
mixture.

Cut the flesh across the grain at a 45° angle into thin slices
with a long sharp knife.

Arrange the slices on chilled plates lined with fresh crisp
lettuce leaves.

Serve the salmon chilled, with green mayonnaise served
separately.

Serves 8

SALMON-STUFFED POTATOES

A splendid way of making use of left-over salmon.

4 large baking potatoes
2 oz/50 g butter, softened
6 tablespoons double cream
8 oz/225 g cooked salmon, boned and flaked
2 eggs, hard-boiled and chopped
1 tablespoon fresh dill, chopped, OR
1 teaspoon dried dill weed
pinch of nutmeg
salt and freshly ground white pepper

Prick the potatoes, dust them with salt and bake them in a moderately hot oven (400°F/300°C/Gas Mark 6) until they are soft right through. It takes approximately 1¾ hours for large potatoes.

When they are cooked, cut them in half without damaging the shells. Scoop out the pulp and mix it in a large bowl with the butter, cream and nutmeg and salt and pepper to taste.

Beat the mixture until it is fluffy, then stir in the salmon, eggs and dill. Mix well and pile the mixture into the empty potato shells.

Bake the shells on a baking sheet in a preheated hot oven at 420°F/230°C/Gas Mark 8 for 10 minutes if they are at room temperature: if they have been prepared earlier, placed in the refrigerator and are cold, bake them for 20 minutes.

Transfer them to warmed plates and serve hot.
Serves 8

SEAFOOD COCKTAIL

1¾ pint/1 litre chicken stock
1 bay leaf
6 peppercorns
2 tablespoons white wine
3½ oz/100 g white fish
2 fillets of sole
½ pint/300 ml mayonnaise, see page 266
2 oz/50 g cooked shrimps, peeled

a few shrimps for garnish
salt
chopped parsley

Combine the chicken stock, bay leaf, peppercorns and white wine in a saucepan and bring to boil. Reduce the heat, add the fish and simmer over low heat for 10-15 minutes.
Remove the fish and allow it to cool.
When completely cold, cut the fish into small pieces, removing any bones.
In a bowl mix very carefully the fish with the shrimps. Spoon over the mayonnaise and blend it gently.
Divide the mixture into 4 chilled dishes, garnish with chopped parsley and the remaining shrimps. Serve chilled.
Serves 4

SARDINE COCKTAIL

1 tin sardines in oil, drained
1 egg, hard-boiled
3 tablespoons spring onions, finely chopped
1 stalk celery, finely chopped
5 oz/150 g small cooked peas, chilled
mayonnaise, see page 266
few stuffed olives, sliced
salt and pepper
crisp lettuce leaves
lemon wedges

Remove the backbones and the tails of the sardines. In a bowl mash the sardines together with the egg. Stir in the onion, celery and peas. Add enough mayonnaise to hold the mixture together.
Season with salt and pepper and blend well.
Chill, covered, for at least 1 hour.
Serve in mounds in chilled bowls or plates lined with crisp lettuce leaves.
Garnish with stuffed sliced olives and lemon wedges.
Serve chilled.
Serves 4

WHITEBAIT

My husband's favourite starter. But only if the whitebait are crisp.

1 pint/600 ml fresh whitebait
seasoned flour
oil for deep frying
cayenne pepper
lemon wedges

Pick over the whitebait, but don't wash them. Roll a small quantity at a time lightly in seasoned flour.
Heat a deep fat fryer and add the oil.
Put a handful of floured whitebait in the frying basket and plunge it into the oil for 2-3 minutes. Drain the whitebait on absorbent kitchen paper.
Continue the frying process until all the whitebait are fried.
Reheat the oil until a faint blue haze rises. Put all the whitebait into the basket, and plunge it into the oil for a further 1-2 minutes, or until they are crisp.
Serve hot with lemon wedges and dusted with cayenne pepper.
Serves 4

TURBOT VOL-AU-VENTS

1 lb/450 g turbot, or any other firm-fleshed white fish
5 oz/150 g butter
juice of 1 lemon
8 small, or 4 large, baked vol-au-vent cases
4 egg yolks
¼ teaspoon sugar
1½ teaspoons paprika
salt

Skin the fish, remove all bones and cut it into small pieces.
Place the fish in an ovenproof dish together with 1 oz/25 g of the butter and half of the lemon juice.
Cover and cook in a cool oven (300°F/150°C/Gas Mark 2) for 15 minutes.
Heat the vol-au-vent cases in the oven.

In a bowl whisk the egg yolks with the remaining lemon juice, sugar, paprika, salt and 4 tablespoons of water.

Place the bowl over a larger pan of boiling water and continue to whisk until the mixture begins to thicken.

Melt the remaining butter and add it gradually to the mixture.

Continue to whisk until the butter is complete absorbed.

Fill the vol-au-vent cases with the flaked fish and spoon the sauce over the fish. Serve immediately.

Serves 4

POISSON CRU

An aromatic speciality from the South Sea Islands.
But it must be arranged attractively, or it can look a little pallid.

2 lb/900 g fresh turbot, skinned, boned and diced
6 tablespoons fresh lime juice
9 oz/250 g cucumber, peeled, seeded and diced
3 tomatoes, peeled, seeded and chopped
1 onion, thinly sliced
1 green pepper, seeded and thinly sliced
coconut cream from 2 coconuts
8 lettuce leaves
salt
2 eggs, hard-boiled and quartered
8 small gherkins
sprigs of parsley

In a glass bowl combine the turbot with the lime juice and salt to taste. Cover, and marinate it in a cool place for at least 4 hours. Stir it occasionally with a wooden spoon.

Drain the turbot, place it in a large bowl and add the cucumber, tomatoes, onion, green pepper and coconut cream.

Line 8 chilled serving plates with the lettuce leaves and top each of them with the turbot mixture.

Garnish each portion with egg quarters, gherkins and parsley sprigs.

Serve chilled

Serves 8

TUNA SALAD NIÇOISE

9 oz/250 g French green beans, cooked
2 eggs, hard-boiled and shelled
3 tomatoes, peeled, seeded and quartered
crisp leaves of 1 lettuce
1 clove of garlic, crushed
1 (8 oz/225 g) tin of tuna, drained and flaked
2 oz/50 g black olives
4 tablespoons French dressing, see page 265
salt and freshly ground black pepper
2 oz/50 g tinned anchovy fillets, drained

Line a large salad bowl with the lettuce leaves.
Fill it with the beans, eggs, tomatoes, garlic, tuna and most
of the olives. Pour over the dressing and toss lightly.
Season with salt and freshly ground black pepper.
Garnish with the remaining olives and anchovy fillets.
Serve cold accompanied by crusty hot French bread.
Serves 4-6

CAESAR SALAD

This is a very filling salad and can almost be a meal in itself.

1 clove of garlic
6 fl oz/150 ml olive oil
8 slices of crustless white bread, cut into small cubes
½ teaspoon salt
freshly ground black pepper
2 eggs, boiled for 1 minute
juice of 1 lemon
6-8 anchovy fillets, drained and chopped
1 oz/25 g Parmesan cheese, grated
2 large heads of cos lettuce, washed and patted dry

In a small bowl crush the garlic, pour over the olive oil and
leave for several hours.
In a heavy frying-pan heat some of the oil and garlic.
Brown the small bread cubes, turning frequently to avoid
burning. When golden brown, turn off the heat and keep

warm in the pan.

Tear the lettuce into a large salad bowl, sprinkle with salt, the remaining garlic oil and a generous amount of freshly ground black pepper. Toss until every leaf is glossy.

Break in the eggs, boiled previously for 1 minute, squeeze over the lemon juice and toss thoroughly.

Add the anchovies and the Parmesan and toss again.

With a slotted spoon remove the bread cubes *(croûtons)* from the pan and add just before serving.

Toss gently, serve immediately on cold plates.
Serves 8-10

CHOPPED HERRING

2 salt herrings
1 thick slice white bread
2 tablespoons wine vinegar
1 egg, hard-boiled
1 apple, peeled, cored and quartered
1 small onion, finely grated
2 tablespoons vegetable oil
freshly ground white pepper
crisp lettuce leaves

Soak the herrings in cold water for 24 hours, changing the water at least twice.

Wash the herrings, pat them dry and remove the heads, the tails, and the bones. Chop the herrings into small pieces.

Cut off the crust and soak the bread in vinegar. When most of the liquid has been absorbed, mash the bread with a fork.

Separate the egg yolk from the white. Chop the egg yolk very finely and set aside for garnish.

In a large bowl combine the apple, egg white, herring and bread. Mix well, then chop the mixture very finely. Blend in the vegetable oil, grated onion and pepper. Mix well.

Serve on lettuce leaves sprinkled with egg yolk.

Serve cold.
Serves 4

ROLLMOPS

6 salt herrings
3 tablespoons German sweet brown mustard
1½ tablespoons capers, drained
2 small onions, sliced thinly and separated into rings
3 small dill gherkins, quartered lengthwise

for the marinade
½ pint/300 ml tarragon vinegar
2 tablespoons sugar
3 bay leaves
10 white peppercorns
3 juniper berries
4 cloves
4 whole allspice
1½ teaspoons mustard seed
1 tablespoon fresh dill, chopped, OR
1 teaspoon dill weed
1 large onion, sliced and separated into rings.

Rinse the herrings under running cold water. Place them in a shallow bowl, cover with water and soak overnight.
Rinse the herrings again under running cold water. Remove the heads, the tails, the fins, and fillet the herrings, leaving the skin intact. Pat the fillets dry.
Spread the insides of the fillets with the mustard, add the capers and small onion rings and place a piece of gherkin across the end of each fillet. Roll the fillet up and secure the rolls with wooden picks.

To make the marinade
In a stainless steel or enamel saucepan combine ¾ pint/ 450 ml water, the vinegar, sugar, bay leaves, peppercorns, juniper berries, cloves, allspice and mustard seed. Bring this mixture to the boil and continue boiling for 5 minutes. Let it cool until it is lukewarm.

Put the dill and half of the large onion rings in the bottom of a shallow glass dish large enough to hold the rolls in one layer. Top the rolls with the remaining onion rings and pour

over the marinade. Chill in refrigerator, covered, for 3 days.
Turn the rolls once a day. Serve cold with dark rye bread.
Serves 12

BOMBAY HERRING

6 herrings with soft roes
1 bay leaf
lemon zest
8 black peppercorns
1 small onion, sliced
½ pint/300 ml mayonnaise, see page 266
2 teaspoons curry powder
1 small eating apple, peeled, cored and chopped
thinly sliced rye bread
½ pint/300 ml water

Fillet, skin and scale the herrings. Roll each fillet round a
soft roe. Preheat the oven to 325°F/160°C/Gas Mark 3.
Place the rolled herrings into a slightly greased ovenproof
dish. Pour over the water, add the onion, lemon zest, bay
leaf and peppercorns. Cover and cook for 30 minutes. Cool,
then drain.
Mix the curry powder with the mayonnaise and chopped
apple. Arrange the herrings on a serving platter and spread
them with the mayonnaise and curry mixture.
Serve cold with thinly sliced buttered rye bread.
Serves 6

HERRING WITH DILL AND TOMATO

4 fillets of salt herrings
3 tablespoons olive oil
1 tablespoon white wine vinegar
1 tablespoon water
1 tablespoon concentrated tomato purée
freshly ground white pepper
1 tablespoon sugar
1 tablespoon fresh dill, chopped, OR
1¼ teaspoons dried dill weed

Soak the herrings overnight in a shallow dish filled with water.
Drain and rinse the fillets under running cold water. Pat them dry.
Slice each fillet diagonally in ½ inch/1 cm strips. Place them in a flat glass or earthenware dish.
In a bowl blend the oil, vinegar, water, tomato purée, pepper, sugar and dill. Spoon the mixture over the fish and chill, covered, in the refrigerator, for at least 3 hours.
Serve chilled.
Serves 4-6

MARINATED KIPPER FILLETS

This is an inexpensive version of marinated smoked salmon. And it's just as delicious!

8 oz/225 g boned kipper fillets, fresh or frozen
4 tablespoons vegetable oil
juice of 1 lemon
1 onion, finely sliced
1 teaspoon dried dill weed
1 bay leaf
freshly ground black pepper

If frozen, defrost the fillets.
Skin the fillets and put them into a shallow dish.
In a separate bowl mix the oil, lemon juice, onion, dill, bay leaf and black pepper. Blend this mixture well, pour it over

the fillets, turning them so that they are well coated.
Chill the fillets, covered, in the refrigerator for 24 hours.
Serve chilled accompanied by hot toast.
Serves 4

SOFT ROES WITH CREAM AND WINE

12 oz/350 g soft herring roes
2 bay leaves
5 white peppercorns
2 tablespoons lemon juice
1 shallot, finely chopped
3 tablespoons medium dry white wine
¾ pint/450 ml double cream
salt and pepper
chopped parsley

Place the herring roes, bay leaves, peppercorns and lemon
juice into a shallow frying-pan. Add enough water to cover
the roes. Cook them gently over low heat for 4-6 minutes.
Drain the roes and discard the liquid.
Put the finely chopped shallot into a small saucepan and add
the white wine. Simmer until the wine has almost boiled
away.
Stir in the cream and simmer gently for a further few
minutes.
Season with salt and pepper. Add the roes and gently heat
them through.
Cover, and leave to cool. Chill, covered, in the refrigerator
for at least 3 hours.
Sprinkle with chopped parsley.
Serves 4-6

Shellfish

PRAWN COCKTAIL

8 oz/225 g prawns, cooked and peeled
2 tablespoons mayonnaise, see page 266
1 tablespoon tomato ketchup
dash of tabasco sauce
dash of Worcestershire sauce
pinch of celery salt
salt and freshly ground black pepper
lemon wedges
crisp lettuce leaves, shredded

Arrange the lettuce in the bottom of 4 individual glasses or dishes. Pile the prawns on the top.
In a separate bowl combine the mayonnaise, tomato ketchup, tabasco sauce, Worcestershire sauce, celery salt and salt and pepper. Blend it into a smooth cream and spoon it over the prawns.
Garnish with lemon wedges.
Chill for at least 30 minutes.
Served chilled
Serves 4

PRAWN AND MELON COCKTAIL

½ small melon for each person
6 large prawns, cooked and peeled, for each person
mayonnaise, see page 266
pinch of cayenne pepper
¼ teaspoon dried dill
crisp lettuce leaves, shredded
salt and freshly ground black pepper

Remove the seeds from the melon halves.

In a large bowl mix the prawns with the mayonnaise, cayenne pepper, dill, salt and freshly ground black pepper.

Stand each half melon in a bowl of cracked ice. Fill the hollow of the melon with the prawn mixture.

Serve very chilled.

PRAWNS IN HORSERADISH MAYONNAISE

1 lb/450 g prawns, cooked and shelled
¾ pint/450 ml mayonnaise, see page 266
1 large green pepper, seeded and finely chopped
1 medium onion, finely chopped
3 tablespoons horseradish sauce
1 teaspoon sweet paprika
salt and pepper to taste
chopped parsley

In a large bowl mix the mayonnaise with the horseradish, onion and green pepper. Blend well, then add the prawns and salt and pepper to taste.

Chill, covered, in the refrigerator for at least 1 hour.

Serve in chilled glasses or bowls, sprinkled with parsley and dusted with paprika.

Serves 4-6

PRAWN AND CELERY REMOULADE

4 stalks celery
8 tablespoons mayonnaise, see page 266
4 spring onions, finely chopped
2 teaspoons Dijon mustard
2 teaspoons parsley, finely chopped
2 teaspoons lemon juice
pinch of cayenne pepper
pinch of sugar
salt and pepper to taste
8 oz/225 g prawns, cooked and peeled
crisp lettuce leaves

Cut the celery into fine *julienne* strips about 2 inches/8 cm long. Place in iced water for at least 30 minutes, or until very crisp. Drain in a colander.
In a bowl combine the mayonnaise, spring onions, mustard, parsley, lemon juice, cayenne, sugar, salt and pepper. Mix well, then fold in the celery and the prawns.
Chill, covered, for at least 2 hours.
Divide the mixture between 4 chilled plates lined with lettuce leaves. Serve chilled.
Serves 4

PRAWNS IN MUSTARD AND ONION SAUCE

1 lb/450 g prawns, peeled
4 fl oz/100 ml dry white wine
1 small onion, sliced
½ carrot, chopped
½ stalk of celery, chopped
¼ teaspoon salt
12 black peppercorns
½ pint/300 ml mayonnaise, see page 266
2 tablespoons Dijon mustard
½ onion, finely grated
crisp lettuce leaves
4 lemon wedges
parsley sprigs

In a heavy saucepan combine the prawns, wine, onion, carrot, celery, salt and peppercorns. Cook, covered over moderate heat for 10 minutes. Drain the prawns, discarding the liquid. Leave to cool.

In a bowl combine the mayonnaise and the mustard. Mix well, then add the prawns and the grated onion.

Chill, covered loosely, in the refrigerator for 4 hours.

Serve on chilled plates lined with lettuce leaves. Garnish with lemon wedges and parsley sprigs.

Serves 4

PRAWNS WITH TEQUILA SAUCE

A good way of getting any dinner party off the ground.

16 large prawns, cooked but unpeeled

for the sauce
1 egg yolk
1 whole egg
1 teaspoon Dijon mustard
1 tablespoon cider- or white wine vinegar
½ teaspoon salt
7 oz/200 ml vegetable oil
7 oz/200 ml mild pickled pimentos
6 tablespoons Tequila
1 teaspoon bottled chilli sauce
few drops angostura bitters
few drops tabasco sauce

Arrange the prawns on individual plates and chill.

In an electric blender or mixer blend the whole egg, egg yolk, mustard, vinegar and salt. With the motor running add the oil in a slow stream; then add the pimentos, Tequila, chilli sauce, angostura bitters, and tabasco sauce.

Blend until all ingredients are well mixed.

Serve the sauce separately in a sauce-boat accompanying the prawns.

Serve cold.

Serves 4-6

BAKED PRAWNS WITH PAPAYA

2 papayas, not too soft
8 oz/225 g prawns, cooked and peeled
juice of half a lemon
½ pint/300 ml béchamel sauce, see page 270
1 egg yolk
pinch of powdered ginger
1 oz/25 g toasted breadcrumbs
½ oz/15 g butter
salt and pepper

Peel the papayas, halve them and remove the stones. Gently scoop out the flesh and dice it. Reserve the shells. Sprinkle the flesh with lemon juice.

Make the béchamel sauce. Add the prawns, papayas and the powdered ginger. Heat through, then add the lightly beatened egg yolk. Serve and simmer over very low heat for not longer than a minute.

Pile the mixture into the 4 half shells of the papayas.

Sprinkle with toasted breadcrumbs and put a small dot of butter into the centre of each serving. Bake in the oven for 15 minutes (350°F/180°C/Gas Mark 4). Serve hot.
Serves 4

PRAWNS IN GARLIC

1½ lb/675 g plump and juicy prawns, in their shells
1 tablespoon olive oil
1 oz/25 g butter
2-3 cloves of garlic, according to taste, crushed
pinch of cayenne pepper
1 tablespoon whisky or brandy
hot crusty French bread

In a heavy frying-pan heat the oil and the butter. Add the garlic, stir, and cook for 1 minute, then add the prawns. Cook, stirring, for 3-4 minutes until thoroughly heated.

Sprinkle with cayenne and pour over the whisky or brandy.

Set alight and serve, while still flaming, with any juices from

the pan poured over the prawns.
Serve accompanied by hot crusty French bread.
Serves 4

CREOLE PRAWNS HORS D'OEUVRE

4 oz/100 g prawns, cooked and shelled
2 chilli peppers, seeded and finely chopped
2 teaspoons lemon juice
1 tablespoon olive oil
¼ teaspoon salt
bread, toast or savoury biscuits

Chop the prawns and combine them with the chillis, lemon juice, oil and salt in a mortar. Pound the mixture into a smooth paste. Pile on small pieces of bread, toast or savoury biscuits. Serve cold.
Serves 2-4

POTTED PRAWNS

8 oz/250 g prawns, cooked and peeled
2 oz/50 g unsalted butter
¼ teaspoon ground mace
¼ small nutmeg, finely grated
cayenne pepper
salt
2 oz/50 g clarified butter

Rinse the prawns in cold water and pat them dry with kitchen paper towel.
Melt the unsalted butter, add mace and nutmeg. Lower the heat and gently stir in the prawns until they have absorbed the butter. Do not overheat them, or they will toughen. Season the prawns with cayenne pepper and a little salt.
Spoon the mixture into 4 ramekins.
Melt the clarified butter and pour it over the prawns. Cool, then cover and chill for several hours. Serve cold with hot toast.
Serves 4

LOBSTER COCKTAIL

6 oz/175 g lobster meat
4 tablespoons mayonnaise, see page 266
4 tablespoons tomato ketchup
cayenne pepper
pinch of celery salt
salt and white pepper
1 lettuce heart, shredded
4 lemon slices

Flake the lobster meat roughly.
Blend the mayonnaise with the tomato ketchup, celery salt, cayenne, salt and white pepper.
Divide the shredded lettuce among 4 cocktail glasses or small glass dishes.
Fold the lobster meat into the mayonnaise, mix well and spoon an equal portion into each glass or dish. Hook a lemon slice onto each rim and dust the lobster cocktail with a little cayenne pepper.
Serve chilled.
Serves 4

CRAB TARTARE

1 lb/450 g light crabmeat, cooked
1 tablespoon toasted breadcrumbs
1 oz/25 g butter, melted

for the sauce
½ pint/300 ml béchamel sauce, see page 270
2 teaspoons capers, chopped
2 teaspoons gherkins, chopped
1 tablespoon parsley, chopped
2 tablespoons double cream
1 egg yolk, lightly beaten
salt and pepper

Flake the crabmeat. In a saucepan combine the béchamel sauce, crabmeat, capers, gherkins and parsley. Mix well and heat through; then add the cream and the lightly beaten egg yolk. Stir and heat without boiling.

Pour the mixture into an ovenproof dish and sprinkle with breadcrumbs. Brush with melted butter and brown it under a hot grill.

Serve hot.

Serves 4-6

CRAB GUMBO

8 oz/225 g crabmeat, flaked
2 eggs, hard-boiled
1 oz/25 g butter, melted
1 oz/25 g flour
juice of 1 lemon
rind of 1 lemon, finely grated
½ pint/300 ml milk
4 tablespoons single cream
salt and black pepper
2 tablespoons medium dry sherry
dash of Angostura bitters

In a heavy saucepan over medium heat mash the eggs into a paste and combine them with the melted butter. Add the flour, lemon juice and rind.

In a separate saucepan heat the milk. Just before boiling point take it off the heat. Gradually stir in the egg mixture and continue to stir until it is smooth.

Return the mixture to the heat, and bring to the boil, stirring constantly. Simmer very gently for 5 minutes. Remove it from the heat and, briskly, stir in the cream, add the flaked crabmeat, salt and pepper to taste, sherry and bitters.

Heat through without boiling.

Serve hot.

Serves 4-6

QUICK CRABMEAT BISQUE

One of my most favourite stand-by soup recipes. It's quick and very easy and tastes just like the real thing.

2 (10.6 oz/300 g) tins concentrated tomato soup
2 (10.6 oz/300 g) tins concentrated green pea soup
1 (7 oz/198 g) tin crabmeat, with the liquid
¼ teaspoon curry powder
3 tablespoons medium dry sherry
1 pint/600 ml cold water
1 (5 fl oz/150 ml) carton single cream
chopped parsley for garnish

In a large saucepan combine all the ingredients except for the sherry and the cream.
Stir well and bring to the boil. Reduce the heat, simmer for 3 minutes, stirring frequently; then add the cream and the sherry.Serve immediately, each portion sprinkled with chopped parsley.
Serves 6-8

CRÈME DE ST JACQUES

8 oz/225 g scallops, cleaned and chopped
2½ pints/1.5 litres water
¾ lb/340 g potatoes, peeled and quartered
2 medium onions, chopped
1 bay leaf
¾ teaspoon dried thyme
salt to taste
freshly ground black pepper
¼ teaspoon garlic salt
2 egg yolks
5 fl oz/142 ml double cream

In a large saucepan boil the water, add the potatoes, onions, bay leaf, thyme, salt and pepper.
Simmer, covered, for 50 minutes. Add the chopped scallops and cook 5 minutes longer over high heat, without the lid.
Reduce the heat, add the garlic salt and remove the bay leaf.

Rub the soup through a coarse sieve, then return it to the saucepan and bring to boil. Take off the heat and stir in the egg yolks, blended with the cream.
Gently reheat, but do not boil again.
Serve hot in warmed soup bowls.
Serves 6-8

SCALLOPS ST JACQUES

1¾ pints/1 litre chicken stock
1 bay leaf
6 black peppercorns
2 tablespoons dry white wine
8 large scallops with their corals
1 clove of garlic, crushed
1 shallot, chopped
3½ oz/100 g butter
5 oz/150 g small button mushroom, chopped
flour
3 tablespoons double cream
1¾ oz/50 g Gruyère cheese, grated
toasted breadcrumbs

In a large saucepan combine the chicken stock, bay leaf, peppercorns and white wine. Bring to boil, then reduce heat. Add the scallops and their corals, and simmer over very low heat for 3-5 minutes. Drain carefully, reserving the liquid.
In a separate saucepan cook the garlic and the shallot in half of the butter. Add the mushrooms and simmer.
In another saucepan melt the remaining butter and stir in some flour. Stir, adding the reserved liquid in a slow stream. Continue stirring until the sauce is smooth and thick.
Add the scallops, garlic and mushrooms to the sauce.
Blend carefully, then add the cream.
Pour the mixture into individual scallop shells, or ovenproof dishes. Sprinkle with toasted breadcrumbs and cheese. Dot each serving with a little butter.
Brown under the grill or cook in a moderate oven at 325°F/160°C/Gas Mark 3 for 15 minutes. Serve immediately.
Serves 4

SCALLOPS WITH AVOCADO AND RED PEPPER SAUCE

1½ lb/675 g scallops, washed and sliced horizontally
6 tablespoons lemon juice
salt and white pepper
3 large avocados
1½ lb/675 g red peppers
2 tablespoons olive oil
cayenne pepper

In a glass bowl combine the lemon juice, scallops, salt and white pepper. Toss well, cover the bowl tightly and marinate overnight. The lemon juice will 'cook' the scallops.
Drain the scallops.
Peel, halve lengthwise and stone the avocados.
Halve again, then slice each quarter, keeping one end attached. Brush the avocados with lemon juice.
To make the sauce
Put the red peppers under a hot grill, turning frequently for 10 minutes, or until the skins are charred. Leave to cool.
Over a bowl, discard stems, seeds and skins.
Chop the peppers coarsely, put them into an electric blender or mixer and purée. With the motor running add the oil, cayenne pepper, salt and white pepper. Blend until smooth. Add more oil if you wish.
Divide the red pepper sauce among 12 salad plates. Divide the avocados equally, arranging them in a fan-like shape over the sauce. Top it with the marinated scallops.
Serve cold.
Serves 12

Mussels

To Clean Mussels
Scrub the mussels in several changes of water. Scrape each shell with a knife, removing all traces of mud and barnacles. The shells should be tightly closed. Discard any which are even slightly open.

To Steam Mussels
Put the mussels into a saucepan with very little water and cover tightly with the lid. Cook gently until the shells open. Strain the liquor and keep it for the sauce.
Remove any weed there may be under the black tongue.
Discard any which fail to open.

To Keep Cooked Mussels
Wrap the mussels in a damp towel and put them on the lowest shelf of the refrigerator.

To Keep Raw Mussels
Put in a container, with water midway, in the refrigerator; sprinkle with a tablespoon of flour to provide nourishment.

Cleaning and preparing mussels

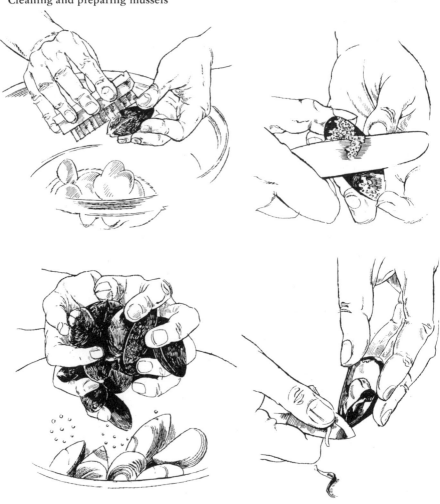

MOULES MARINIÈRE

4-6 dozen mussels
2 oz/50 g butter
4 shallots, finely chopped
½ pint/300 ml dry white wine
3 tablespoons parsley, chopped
1 bay leaf
salt and freshly ground black pepper

Clean the mussels as directed on page 145.

In a large saucepan sauté the shallots in the butter until they are transparent. Add the wine, parsley, bay leaf, black pepper and salt to taste. Simmer over low heat for 10 minutes.

Add the mussels, cover the saucepan tightly and steam, shaking constantly, until the mussel shells open.

Remove the top shells, but leave each mussel attached to the lower shell. Arrange the mussels in a large deep serving platter and keep warm.

Reduce the liquid by half by boiling it vigorously and correct the seasoning. Serve immediately.

Serves 4-6

DEVILLED MUSSELS

5 lb/2.27 kg mussels, cleaned, steamed open and shelled
1 medium onion, chopped
1 small green pepper, seeded and chopped
1 small red pepper, seeded and chopped
4 tablespoons celery, finely chopped
3 oz/75 g butter
1 tablespoon Dijon mustard
cayenne pepper to taste
salt
2 oz/50 g toasted breadcrumbs

In a heavy saucepan cook the onion, the green and red peppers and the celery in 2 oz/50 g of the butter over moderate heat for 3 minutes, or until the vegetables are just tender.

Remove the pan from the heat and stir in the mussels, mustard, cayenne pepper and salt to taste. Mix well, then divide the mixture between 4 buttered ovenproof dishes. Sprinkle with breadcrumbs and dot the tops with the remaining 1 oz/25 g of butter.

Bake in a preheated oven (400°F/200°C/Gas Mark 6) for 6-8 minutes, or until the crumbs are browned.

Serve hot.

Serves 4

MUSSELS IN DILLED CUCUMBER SAUCE

5 lb/2.27 kg mussels, cleaned, steamed open and shelled
8 tablespoons cucumber, peeled, seeded and chopped
¼ pint/150 ml sour cream
3 tablespoons fresh dill, finely chopped, OR
1 tablespoon dried dill weed
1 teaspoon lemon juice
1 teaspoon Dijon mustard
3-6 drops tabasco sauce
salt and freshly ground white pepper
crisp lettuce leaves

In a large bowl combine the cucumber, sour cream, dill, lemon juice, mustard, tabasco sauce, white pepper and salt to taste.
Add the mussels and toss the mixture well. Serve it on chilled plates lined with lettuce leaves.
Serve very cold.
Serves 4

MUSSEL AND CELERIAC SALAD

3 lb/1.35 kg mussels, cleaned, steamed open and shelled
1 lb/450 g celeriac, peeled and grated
8 oz/225 g mayonnaise, see page 266
2 tablespoons Dijon mustard
2 tablespoons gherkin, finely chopped
2 tablespoons parsley, finely chopped
1 tablespoon lemon juice
2 tablespoons double cream
salt and freshly ground black pepper

In a saucepan of boiling salted water blanch the celeriac for 1 minute. Drain in a colander and pat dry.
In a salad bowl combine the mayonnaise, mustard, gherkin, parsley, lemon juice, cream and salt and pepper to taste. Blend, add the mussels and the celeriac, and toss well.
Serve very cold.
Serves 4-6

MUSSELS AND ARTICHOKE VINAIGRETTE

2 (5 oz/150 g) jars cooked mussels, drained
14 oz/400 g tinned artichoke hearts, drained
8 oz/225 g courgettes, thickly sliced
½ small cauliflower, divided into florettes
2 rashers lean bacon
3 fl oz/80 ml French dressing, see page 265

Steam the courgettes and the cauliflower in a little water for 8 minutes. Drain and leave to cool.
Grill or fry the bacon until it is very crisp. Drain on absorbent kitchen paper, then crumble it.
On a serving platter arrange the courgettes, cauliflower, artichokes and mussels. Sprinkle with the bacon and spoon the French dressing over the dish.
Serve very cold.
Serves 4-6

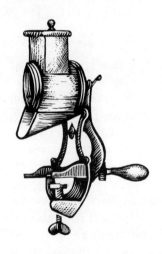

Fish Mousse and Pâté

SALMON MOUSSE

1 lb/450 g cooked salmon, or salmon trout
1 oz/25 g butter
1 oz/25 g flour
2 large eggs, separated
¼ pint/150 ml fish stock (from the salmon)
¼ pint/150 ml double cream, whipped
1 tablespoon lemon juice
2 tablespoons tomato paste
½ oz/15 g powdered gelatine
3 tablespoons warm water
cucumber slices for garnish

Mash the salmon pieces with a fork.
Melt the butter in a saucepan and stir in the flour. Cook for
1 minute, then remove from the heat and slowly pour in the
fish stock, stirring. Return to the heat, bring to boil, stirring
constantly, then simmer for 2 minutes.
Let the sauce cool slightly. Beat the egg yolks and stir them,
together with the lemon juice, cream and tomato paste, into
the cooling sauce.
Stir in the fish.
Dissolve the gelatine in the water in a basin over a pan of
simmering water. Whisk it into the salmon mixture.
Beat the egg whites until they are stiff. Fold them into the
salmon and pour the mixture into a large soufflé dish, or
into individual small dishes. Cool, then chill for several
hours. Garnish with cucumber slices and serve with hot
toast.
Serve chilled.
Serves 6-8

TUNA AND COD MOUSSE

½ oz/15 g powdered gelatine
2 tablespoons water
1 (7 oz/200 g) tin tuna, drained and mashed
6 oz/175 g cooked cod, boned and mashed
½ pint/300 ml mayonnaise, see page 266
dash of tabasco sauce
1 (6 oz/170 g) tin evaporated milk, chilled
1 tablespoon lemon juice

2 teaspoons oil
1 lb/450 g tomatoes, peeled and quartered
2 teaspoons lemon juice
6 spring onions, finely chopped
cucumber slices
radish slices
salt and pepper

Dissolve the gelatine in the water in a basin over a pan of boiling water. In a bowl combine the tuna with the cod. Mash with a fork and add the mayonnaise.
Season with a few drops of tabasco, salt and pepper.
Stir in the gelatine which must be completely dissolved.
Whisk the evaporated milk with 1 tablespoon lemon juice until it thickens, then fold it into the fish mixture.
Pour the mixture into a rinsed ring mould, or a shallow dish, and chill until set.
When the mousse is completely set, dip the mould briefly into hot water, run a thin knife around the edge of the mousse, and invert a serving plate over it. Turn the mousse onto the plate.
Mix together the oil and the lemon juice and toss the tomatoes and spring onions in the dressing. Add salt and pepper and fill the centre of the mould with the tomatoes.
Garnish with slices of cucumber and radishes.
Serve chilled.
Serves 4

SARDINE MOUSSE

1 tin sardines in oil
¾ pint/450 ml chicken stock
1 (0.4 oz/11g) envelope powdered gelatine, or 3 teaspoons
4 eggs, hard-boiled
¼ pint/150 ml mayonnaise, see page 266
1 teaspoon curry powder
¼ pint/150 ml double cream, slightly whipped
1 tablespoon tomato ketchup
6 drops tabasco sauce
1 tablespoon parsley, chopped
salt and pepper

Remove the tails and backbones from the sardines. Keep the oil.

Soften the gelatine in a little cold stock. Bring the remaining stock to boil, add to the gelatine and stir until the gelatine has dissolved. Leave to cool.

Mix the mayonnaise with the curry powder and parsley.

Chop the eggs very finely and put them in a bowl with the sardines. With a fork mash the eggs together with the sardines. Add the tomato ketchup, the oil from the sardine tin, tabasco, curry mayonnaise and salt and pepper. Mix well, then add the slightly whipped cream.

Blend, and when the stock begins to set, beat ½ pint/300 ml into the mixture. Leave it for 30 minutes in a cool place, then beat it again, so that the mixture is light.

Pour the mousse into a soufflé dish, or into individual small dishes, and put it in the refrigerator to set.

Melt the remaining ¼ pint/100 ml of jellied stock and pour it over the mousse. Chill again until it is ready to serve.

Serves 4

SMOKED FISH PÂTÉ

2 smoked trout or mackerel
¼ pint/150 ml sour cream
4 oz/100 g cottage cheese
juice of half a lemon
salt and freshly ground white pepper
¼ teaspoon cayenne pepper
lemon wedges

Skin the fish, remove all bones and chop the flesh finely.
Put it into an electric blender or mixer together with the sour cream, cottage cheese, lemon juice, salt, white pepper and cayenne pepper. Blend at high speed until very smooth.
Spoon into small individual dishes and chill, covered, overnight.
Serve with lemon wedges and thin slices of brown bread or toast.
Serves 4-6

KIPPER PÂTÉ

4 kipper fillets, skinned
juice and zest of 1 lemon
¼ pint/150 ml sour cream
1 teaspoon prepared strong horseradish
½ teaspoon Dijon mustard
salt and freshly ground black pepper

Put the flesh of the kipper together with the lemon zest into an electric blender or mixer. Blend coarsely.
Add the sour cream, horseradish, mustard and lemon juice. Blend briefly, add salt and pepper and blend again.
Spoon the mixture into small dishes and chill, covered, for several hours, or overnight.
Serve with hot toast.
Serves 6

CRAB PÂTÉ

8 oz/225 g crabmeat, white and brown
3 oz/75 g butter
2 egg yolks, lightly beaten
1 tablespoon medium dry sherry
2 tablespoons double cream
2 tablespoons Parmesan cheese, finely grated
salt and black pepper
1 teaspoon lemon juice

Mix the white and brown crabmeat. Place it in a saucepan with the butter; heat and stir. Add the lightly beaten egg yolks, sherry and cream. Continue to stir over low heat until the mixture is well blended and thick. Do not boil!
Season with salt and pepper, blend in the cheese and the lemon juice. Pour the mixture into a dish, cover and chill for several hours or overnight.
Serves 6

SMOKED MACKEREL AND DILL PÂTÉ

8 oz/225 g smoked mackerel fillets, skinned
6 teaspoons fresh dill, finely chopped, OR
3 teaspoons dried dill weed
3 teaspoons lemon juice
1 egg white, stiffly beaten
¼ pint/150 ml double cream, lightly whipped
salt and freshly ground white pepper
lemon and cucumber slices for garnish

Flake the fish, place it in an electric blender or mixer together with the dill, lemon juice and white pepper.
Blend until smooth, then pour the mixture into a bowl.
Add the egg white and the cream, stir well and correct the seasoning. Spoon the mixture into individual ramekin dishes and chill for a few hours, or overnight.
Garnish with slices of cucumber and lemon. Serve cold with brown toast.
Serves 4-6

SMOKED MACKEREL AND GOOSEBERRY PÂTÉ

Mackerel and gooseberries have been combined in cooking for centuries: the Normans served mackerel with gooseberry sauce. This recipe for a smooth and tart pâté is easy to prepare and the result is delicious.

½ lb/225 g gooseberries
1 heaped teaspoon castor sugar
1 tablespoon water
2 smoked mackerel, skinned and boned
2 oz/50 g butter
1 tablespoon Calvados
freshly ground black pepper

Place the gooseberries, sugar and water in a saucepan. Simmer gently until the gooseberries are soft.
Purée in an electric blender or mixer and leave to cool.
With a fork mash the mackerel with the butter and Calvados. When the gooseberries are cold, blend them into the mixture and season with freshly ground black pepper.
Pour the mixture into a dish and chill it in the refrigerator for several hours, or overnight. Serve cold with hot toast.
Serves 4

SCAMPI PÂTÉ

1½ lb/675 g cooked scampi, peeled
6 oz/175 g butter, softened
3 tablespoons mayonnaise, see page 266
1 dessertspoon fresh chives, chopped
salt and freshly ground black pepper

Chop each scampi into 3-4 pieces. Put the scampi into a large bowl and mix with the butter. Slowly add the mayonnaise and continue to mix.
Add the chives, plenty of black pepper and salt to taste; then put the mixture into individual ramekins and chill, covered, for several hours. Serve cold with brown bread or toast.
Serves 4-6

TARAMASALATA

8 oz/225 g smoked cod's roe, skinned
1 large clove of garlic, crushed
1 slice of white bread, crustless
½ pint/300 ml salad or vegetable oil
3 tablespoons lemon juice
freshly ground white pepper
¼ teaspoon cayenne pepper

Soak the bread in a little water.
Put the garlic and the cod's roe into an electric blender or mixer.
Squeeze out the bread and add it to the cod's roe. Blend until the mixture is very smooth, then add the oil gradually as though you were making mayonnaise. The cod's roe will become creamier and thicker.
Season with white and cayenne pepper and plenty of lemon juice. Blend again.
Serve cold with hot toast.
Serves 4

Fruit

Fruit plays an important part in the human diet. But it was not always considered beneficial to our health, and for centuries physicians warned of the dangers of uncooked fruit.

During medieval times fruit was often blamed for sudden unaccountable illnesses. The sale of fruit was forbidden in 1569, a year of pestilence in England, and during the great plague of 1665 fruit again became the subject of suspicion.

Only in the eighteenth century did a change take place in people's attitudes towards raw fruit. Fresh fruit was excepted by medical men as harmless, perhaps even beneficial food. New theories of diets were established and most fruit was considered helpful in counteracting the alkaline properties of meat, cheese and eggs. But moderation was greatly recommended, for gluttony was still the problem it had always been.

Today fruit is the most important part of our daily diet. It provides important vitamins, acids and salt. Citrus fruit contains a high amount of vitamin C.

Most fresh fruit apart from dates (70 calories per ounce/ 25 g) mangoes (36 calories per ounce/25 g) and bananas (27 calories per ounce/25 g) is very low in calories.

MINTED GRAPE AND MELON COCKTAIL

2 ripe Ogen melons
12 oz/350 g dark grapes, halved and pitted
fresh mint leaves, crushed
sprig of fresh mint

Cut the melons in half and remove the seeds.
Put the crushed mint leaves into the hollow of the melon
halves and spoon in the grapes.
Chill. Serve in chilled glasses garnished with a sprig of mint.
Serves 4

MELON AND GRAPE COCKTAIL WITH VINAIGRETTE AND CREAM

2 medium Cantaloup or Charentais melons
1 lb/450 g seedless green grapes
1 tablespoon fresh mint, chopped

for the dressing
1¾ tablespoons lemon juice
4 teaspoons sugar
pinch of salt
freshly ground black pepper
2 tablespoons vegetable oil
2 fl oz/50 ml single cream

Cut the melons in half and remove the seeds. Scoop out the
flesh with a melon ball cutter. Scrape the shells clean, cut
them into quarters and chill.
In a bowl mix the melon balls with the grapes.
In a separate bowl mix the lemon juice with the sugar, salt
and some freshly ground pepper. Whisk and slowly pour in
the oil, followed by the cream, whisking constantly, so that
the dressing emulsifies and thickens slightly. Spoon the
dressing over the melon balls and the grapes and mix gently,
until it is thoroughly coated with the dressing. Check the
seasoning, cover and chill for several hours.
Just before serving, pile it into the chilled melon shells and

sprinkle the chopped mint over the mixture.
Serve chilled in bowls or glasses.
Serves 4

CANTALOUP AND ONION STARTER

2 Cantaloup melons
2 small mild onions, finely sliced
1 small lettuce, shredded
French dressing, see page 265

Cut the melons in half, remove the seeds and scoop out the
flesh with a melon ball cutter. Chill the melon balls for at
least 1 hour.
Mix the melon balls with the onions and the shredded
lettuce. Add the French dressing to taste and toss the
mixture well.
Serve chilled on chilled plates.
Serves 4-6

GELÉE AU MELON

1½ pints/900 ml consommé
½ pint/300 ml white wine
1 honeydew melon
1 tablespooon tomato purée
5 oz/150 g ham, cut into thin strips

Mix the wine and the tomato purée with the consommé and
heat it to boiling point. Cool it to almost setting point.
Cut the melon in half, remove the seeds and scoop out the
flesh with a teaspoon so that it resembles small eggs.
Spoon them into individual soup cups and pour the cooled
consommé over them. Sprinkle the finely shredded ham over
the top and chill until it is completely set.
Serve chilled.
Serves 6

PEACHES WITH HORSERADISH CREAM

3 large peaches, chilled
¼ pint/150 ml double cream, whipped
1 tablespoon extra-strong horseradish
¼ teaspoon salt
sweet paprika
6 crisp lettuce leaves

Wash the peaches, cut them in half lengthwise and remove stones. Place each peach half on a plate lined with a crisp lettuce leaf.
In a bowl mix the horseradish with the cream and add the salt.
Spoon a generous portion of the horseradish mixture into the hollow centre of each peach half.
Dust with paprika, serve chilled, accompanied by hot triangles of toast.
Serves 6

GRAPEFRUIT MAYONNAISE

2 large grapefruit
4 tablespoons mayonnaise, see page 266
2 hard-boiled eggs, peeled and chopped
4 oz/100 g celery, finely chopped
2 oz/50 g walnuts, crushed
4 oz/100 g prawns, cooked and peeled
salt and freshly ground white pepper
sweet paprika

Cut the grapefruit in half and scoop out all the flesh, reserving any excess juice. Chop the flesh and discard the core and any tough membrane. Reserve the shells.
In a large bowl combine the mayonnaise with the juice. Whisk well, then fold in the celery, prawns, grapefruit flesh, eggs and walnut pieces. Season with salt and pepper, mix well and pile the mixture into the grapefruit shells.
Dust them with a little paprika. Serve very cold.
Serves 4

GRAPEFRUIT WITH RUM

2 grapefruit
¼ pint/150 ml dark rum
sugar to taste

Scoop the pulp from the fruit without damaging the shells. Place the pulp together with the rum and the sugar into a bowl. Leave to marinate for 2 hours.
Heat it through just before serving and pour it back into the shells. Serve hot.
Serves 4

STUFFED PEARS WITH ASPIC MAYONNAISE

3 large pears, peeled and halved
1 (10.4 oz/295 g) tin consommé
¼ pint/150 ml mayonnaise, see page 266
3 pineapple slices, fresh or tinned
6 oz/175 g cream cheese
¼ teaspoon curry powder
a few drops of milk
salt and white pepper
1 tablespoon parsley, finely chopped
shredded lettuce
cayenne pepper

Scoop out the pear cores with a rounded teaspoon.
Blend the consommé with the mayonnaise.
Coarsely chop the pineapple and mix with the cream cheese and the curry powder. Add a few drops of milk if the mixture is not smooth enough. Season with salt and pepper and fill the hollow of the pears with the cream cheese mixture.
On a flat plate place the pears, cut side down, and spoon over the consommé and mayonnaise mixture. Chill in the refrigerator for 2-3 hours, or until completely set.
Line 6 chilled plates with the shredded lettuce and place 1 masked pear on each.
Sprinkle with parsley and dust with cayenne pepper.
Serves 6

MELON MARBLES

1 water melon
¼ pint/150 ml dark rum
juice of 2 oranges
2 tablespoons sugar

Cut the melon in half, remove the seeds and scoop out the flesh with a melon ball cutter.
Place the melon balls, rum, orange juice and sugar in a bowl.
Marinate for at least 3 hours in the refrigerator.
Serve chilled in individual chilled glasses or bowls.
Serves 4-6

LEMONS STUFFED WITH SARDINE MOUSSE

An attractive and festive starter.

4 scooped-out lemon shells
1 (8 oz/225 g) tin sardines in oil
4 oz/100 g butter, softened
4 oz/100 g cream cheese
juice of half a lemon
1 teaspoon Dijon mustard
1 teaspoon capers, drained and finely chopped
salt and freshly ground black pepper
sprigs of dill or parsley for decoration

Remove the backbones and tails from the sardines.
In a bowl mash the sardines in their oil, add the butter and cream cheese and blend well. Beat in the lemon juice, mustard, capers, salt and pepper.
Mix into a smooth paste, then fill the lemon shells with this mixture. Garnish with sprigs of dill or parsley and serve on individual plates.
Chill and serve very cold.
Serves 4

APPLES STUFFED WITH CRABMEAT

4 very red eating apples
1 (7 oz/200 g) tin light crabmeat
2 tablespoons mayonnaise, see page 266
2 tablespoons single cream
juice and finely grated rind of half a lemon
1 stalk of celery, finely chopped
½ tablespoon white wine vinegar
1 tablespoon walnut oil
1 tablespoon vegetable oil
tabasco sauce
salt and white pepper

Polish the washed apples with a soft towel to make them shine. Cut off about ½ inch/1 cm from the top (not the stalk end) of each apple. Scoop out the flesh of most of the apple with a grapefruit knife or a melon ball cutter. Discard the core and the seeds and chop the rest of the flesh.

In a bowl mix the chopped apple flesh with the mayonnaise, cream, grated lemon rind, lemon juice, tabasco, salt and white pepper. Blend well and add the drained and flaked crabmeat. Mix again and add the celery. Fill the apples with this mixture and replace the tops at a slant.

In a bowl mix the oils and the vinegar and season with salt and pepper. Spoon this carefully over the apples to achieve a shiny look.

Chill before serving.

Serves 4

RHUBARB SLAW

2 stems of young rhubarb, pink parts only
4 oz/100 g Dutch cabbage, finely shredded
½ small green pepper, seeded and diced
1 small carrot, grated

for the dressing
6 tablespoons mayonnaise, see page 266
1 tablespoon sour cream
1 tablespoon white wine vinegar
¼ teaspoon lemon juice
¼ teaspoon cayenne pepper
3 teaspoons castor sugar
salt to taste
4 sprigs of mint for garnish

Cut the rhubarb into ½ inch/1 cm long pieces and blanch in boiling water for half a minute.
Drain, cool and mix with the cabbage, pepper and carrot in a large bowl.
In a separate bowl mix the mayonnaise with the sour cream, add the vinegar, lemon juice, cayenne, sugar and add salt to taste. Blend the dressing well and spoon it over the rhubarb mixture.
Toss, and serve in small individual salad bowls garnished with a sprig of mint. Serve very cold.
Serves 4

MANGO WITH PROSCIUTTO

4 large mangoes
12 very thin slices Prosciutto ham
juice of 1 lemon

Peel the mangoes with a stainless steel knife and cut into ½ inch/1 cm slices. Put the slices on a serving platter and sprinkle with the lemon juice. Arrange the slices of Prosciutto loosely folded around the mangoes.
Serve chilled.
Serves 6

RASPBERRIES WITH LIVER

I was served this unique and delicate combination in a restaurant in Munich. In this country raspberry vinegar is obtainable from most delicatessen shops.

7 oz/200 g calves' liver, cut into thin slices
1 shallot, finely chopped
1½ oz/35 g butter
few drops of Worcestershire sauce
¼ teaspoon celery salt
salt and pepper
2 apples (golden delicious), quartered, cores removed
7 oz/200 g raspberries
2 tablespoons dry white wine
3 tablespoons raspberry vinegar
3 tablespoons walnut oil
crisp lettuce leaves

In a heavy pan sauté the liver with the shallot in 1 oz/25 g of the butter for 3 minutes. Remove the liver with a slotted spoon, drain on absorbent kitchen paper and set aside. Season with Worcestershire sauce, celery salt, salt and pepper.

Cut the apple quarters into thin slices and sauté them for 2 minutes in the remaining butter and the butter in which the liver has been cooked. Remove the apple slices with a slotted spoon and cool on absorbent kitchen paper.

Carefully wash and pat dry the raspberries. Very quickly sauté them in the same pan in which the apples and liver have been cooked. With a slotted spoon remove the raspberries and set aside to cool.

In a separate bowl combine the white wine, raspberry vinegar and walnut oil. Blend well and season with salt and pepper.

Carefully put the liver, apple and raspberries into a bowl and pour the dressing over the mixture. Marinate for 15-20 minutes.

Line a serving platter with lettuce leaves and arrange the liver, apple and raspberries on it.

Serve cold.

Serves 4

ORANGE ONION AND OLIVE SALAD

3 medium oranges
1 medium onion, thinly sliced
12 olives, pitted and sliced
4 oz/100 g Roquefort cheese
1 clove of garlic, crushed
¼ pint/150 ml French dressing, see page 265
crisp lettuce leaves

Peel the oranges and cut them into slices crosswise.
In a large bowl combine the oranges, onion and olives.
Toss well.
In a separate bowl mash the Roquefort and stir in the garlic.
Blend well and moisten with French dressing. Blend again,
then pour it over the orange mixture. Cover and chill for at
least 1 hour.
Serve on cold crisp lettuce leaves on chilled individual plates.
Serves 4-6

ANADALUSIAN ORANGE SALAD

5 oz/150 g cold roast beef
4 oz/100 g olives stuffed with pimentos
3 oranges
1 leek, thoroughly washed and cut into thin rings
2 tablespoons double cream
2 tablespoons mayonnaise, see page 266
1 teaspoon Dijon mustard
2 tablespoons dry sherry
1 tablespoon fresh orange juice
few drops tabasco sauce
salt and freshly ground white pepper
crisp cold lettuce leaves
2 oz/50 g walnuts, finely chopped

Cut the roast beef into strips the size of matchsticks.
Drain the olives and cut them into thin slices.
Peel the oranges, remove all membrane and inner skins and
divide them into small segments.

In a large bowl combine the leek, roast beef, olives and orange segments. Mix well.

In a separate bowl whisk the double cream with the mayonnaise, add the mustard, sherry and orange juice, whisking all the time.

Season with tabasco, freshly ground white pepper and salt.

Divide the mixture between 4 salad plates lined with lettuce leaves. Sprinkle each serving with chopped walnuts.

Serve cold.

Serves 4

SWISS GRAPE SALAD

5 oz/150 g Mozzarella cheese
4 oz/100 g Emmental cheese
2 red-skinned apples, quartered, cores removed
1 shallot, grated finely
11 oz/300 g dark grapes, halved and seeded
8 fl oz/225 ml single cream
juice and grated rind of 1 orange
salt and white pepper
2 oz/50 g walnuts, chopped

Cut both cheeses into strips the size of matchsticks.

Cut the apple-quarters into thin slices.

In a large bowl mix the cheeses with the shallot, grapes and apples.

In a separate bowl mix the cream with the orange juice and rind; blend well and add salt and pepper. Set aside for 10-15 minutes, then check seasoning again.

Pile the fruit and cheese mixture into a salad bowl. Pour over the sauce and toss well. Sprinkle with chopped walnuts.

Serve very cold accompanied by dark rye bread and butter.

Serves 4

GRAPE AND PEAR MOULD WITH GINGER

½ pint/300 ml hot water
1 packet lemon flavoured jelly
½ pint/300 ml ginger ale
1 oz/25 g pecan nuts, chopped
1 pear, peeled and diced
3 oz/75 g grapes, halved and seeded
2 teaspoons crystallized ginger, finely chopped
crisp lettuce leaves
mayonnaise (optional)

Put the jelly into a bowl and pour the boiling water over it.
Stir until it is completely dissolved, then add the ginger ale.
Stir well and chill until it just begins to thicken.
Mix together the pear, grapes, nuts and ginger and stir it into
the jelly mixture.
Pour the mixture into 6 individual small moulds and chill
until firm.
Line 6 plates with lettuce leaves and unmould the jellies.
Serve mayonnaise separately, if desired.
Serve chilled.
Serves 6

WALDORF SALAD

*This salad is named after the famous Waldorf Astoria Hotel
in New York. Sometimes Americans substitute peanuts for walnuts.
I prefer the latter.*

6 red-skinned apples
juice of 2 lemons
1 orange
6 stalks of celery
3 oz/75 g walnuts, chopped
mayonnaise, see page 266
crisp lettuce leaves

Peel the orange, divide it into segments, discarding pips and
tough membrane. Cut each segment in half.

Core and dice the apples; sprinkle them with lemon juice.
Slice the celery into ¼ inch/0.5 cm slices.
In a large salad bowl combine the apples, orange, celery and chopped walnuts. Add the mayonnaise and toss the salad well.
Line a salad platter with lettuce leaves and pile the salad on it.
Serve cold with hot crusty French bread.
Serves 4-6

PINEAPPLE RICE SALAD

14 oz/400 g rice, cooked
8 oz/225 g diced pineapple, fresh or tinned
8 oz/225 g cooked ham, cut into small strips
1 cucumber, peeled, seeded and sliced crosswise
4 spring onions, chopped
6 radishes, sliced
crisp lettuce leaves

for the dressing
½ pint/300 ml natural yoghurt
3 tablespoons sour cream
1 tablespoon fresh mint, finely chopped
cayenne pepper
½ teaspoon ground cumin
salt

In a large glass bowl combine the rice, pineapple, ham, cucumber, spring onions, radishes, cayenne and salt to taste.
In a separate bowl blend the yoghurt with the sour cream, add the mint and cumin, a little more cayenne and salt to taste.
Pour the dressing over the salad, toss it well and leave it to stand, covered, in a cool place for 30 minutes.
Line a platter with lettuce leaves and pile the salad on it.
Serve cold.
Serves 4-6

FRUITY CHEESE SALAD

1 small Ogen melon
1 apple
1 small tin mandarin oranges
4½ oz/115 g dark grapes, halved and seeded
1 tablespoon cocktail cherries
7 oz/200 g Gouda cheese, cut into thin slices
2 tablespoons raspberry vinegar
4 fl oz/100 ml double cream
pinch of sugar
freshly ground white pepper

Quarter the melon and remove all seeds. With a sharp knife remove the flesh and cut it into ¼ inch/0.5 cm-wide slices.
Wash, quarter and core the apple, then thinly slice each quarter.
Drain the mandarins, reserving the liquid.
Halve the cocktail cherries and cut the cheese into 1 inch/ 2 cm-wide strips.
In a glass bowl mix the melon, apple, grapes, mandarins, cherries and cheese.
In a separate bowl blend the raspberry vinegar with the mandarin juice, add the sugar and pepper and pour the dressing over the fruit mixture.
Whisk the cream until stiff and, just before ready to serve, fold in the cream and mix well.
Serve very cold.
Serves 4

CURRIED BANANA STARTER

3 medium bananas
1 tablespoon lemon juice
6 oz/175 g cooked rice, chilled
2 tablespoons celery, sliced
3 oz/75 g seedless green grapes
2 oz/50 g salted peanuts, chopped
1 tablespoon fresh chives, finely chopped
2 tablespoons mild tinned pimentos, cut into thin strips
dash of tabasco sauce
salt and pepper
crisp lettuce leaves

for the sauce
¼ pint/150 ml mayonnaise, see page 266
2 tablespoons single cream
1 tablespoon lemon juice
1½ teaspoons curry powder
½ teaspoon powdered English mustard
2 tablespoons chutney, chopped

Cut the bananas into thin slices and sprinkle immediately with lemon juice to avoid discolouration.
In a large bowl combine the bananas, rice, celery, grapes, peanuts, chives, pimentos, tabasco and salt and pepper. Toss gently and chill.
In a separate bowl combine the mayonnaise, cream, lemon juice, curry and mustard. Mix well.
Add the dressing to the salad and mix gently.
Arrange the banana mixture on crisp cold lettuce leaves and top with a small amount of chutney.
Serves 4-6

Leeks

The origin of this hardy vegetable goes back a very long way. It was grown in Egypt at the time of the Pharoahs and later was introduced to the Romans. Nero, who was anxious to deliver his speeches in a clear and sonorous voice, was known to have leek soup every day in the belief that it would help.

The leek has been the Welsh national emblem since 640AD when the Welsh defeated the Saxons and, to avoid attacking each other by mistake, they pinned a leek to their hats during battle.

The leek, known as 'porrum' in Latin, is the favourite of all pottage vegetables. There are many types of leeks grown in Europe, varying from the strong bulbous kind in England to the milder and tender varieties on the Continent. Leeks are not widely popular in the United States.

Leeks contain potassium and vitamin B.
1 oz/25 g of leeks contains 7 calories.

LEEKS VINAIGRETTE

This is also known as 'poor man's asparagus'. Although there is some similarity, leeks have a distinct and aromatic flavour of their own.

12 small young leeks
½ pint/300 ml chicken stock
1 hard-boiled egg, chopped
2 tablespoons white wine vinegar
1 teaspoon Dijon mustard
8 tablespoons olive oil
salt and freshly ground black pepper
2 tablespoons parsley, finely chopped
paprika

Cut off the roots and 2 inches/4 cm of the green part of the leek. Halve the leeks, leaving at least 1 inch/2.5 cm at the root end. Wash the leeks thoroughly, then simmer them in the chicken stock for 8-10 minutes, or until tender.
Drain in a colander, then refresh under running cold water. Drain thoroughly, pressing out all the liquid.
Arrange the leeks in a flat dish in one layer.
In a bowl combine the vinegar with the mustard and salt and whisk in the olive oil until it emulsifies, then add freshly ground black pepper.
Pour the dressing over the leeks and chill, covered, for at least 4 hours, or overnight.
Just before serving, sprinkle the leeks with the chopped hard-boiled egg and parsley. Dust with paprika.
Serve cold.
Serves 4

LEEK COCKTAIL

1 lb/450 g young leeks
2 tablespoons strong chicken stock
1 oz/25 g butter
2 tablespoons dry white wine
5 fl oz/150 ml double cream
2 tablespoons lemon juice
pinch of sugar
salt and freshly ground white pepper
pinch of cayenne pepper

Cut the leeks into ⅛ inch/0.10 cm slices, wash well and dry thoroughly.

In a heavy pan melt the butter; add the leeks and sauté them, stirring gently, until they become transparent.

Mix the white wine with the stock and add it to the leeks. Quickly bring the mixture to boiling point, then remove the leeks with a slotted spoon, place them in a serving dish and allow to cool.

Whisk the cream until it is stiff but not too dry, add the lemon juice, cayenne, sugar, pepper and salt to taste. Pour the dressing over the leeks, mix well and serve immediately. Serve at room temperature.

Serves 4

LEEK SALAD

6 young leeks
6 tomatoes, peeled, seeded and chopped
4 oz/100 g smoked ham, diced
4 eggs, hard-boiled and sliced
French dressing, see page 265
½ teaspoon Dijon mustard

Trim off the roots and 2 inches/5 cm of the green part of the leeks. Wash thoroughly and cut into 1 inch/2.5 cm rounds.
In a salad bowl combine the leeks, tomatoes, ham and eggs. Mix well.
Stir the mustard into the French dressing, blend and pour over the leek mixture. Mix well and chill, covered, for at least 1 hour.
Serve cold in individual chilled glasses or bowls.
Serves 4-6

LEEKS WITH SESAME GARLIC DRESSING

1½ lb/675 g young leeks
1 clove of garlic, crushed
1 teaspoon sesame seeds
¼ pint/150 ml olive oil
2 tablespoons white wine vinegar
1 tablespoon fresh parsley, finely chopped
salt and freshly ground black pepper

Trim the leeks and wash thoroughly. Boil in salted water for 5-6 minutes, or until the green part is just tender. Drain in a colander, refresh under running cold water and cool on absorbent kitchen paper towel. Press out excess moisture and pat the leeks dry.
Arrange the leeks in one layer on a serving platter.
In a heavy saucepan cook the garlic and the sesame seeds in a little oil. Stir until the seeds are golden.
In a small bowl combine the vinegar, salt and pepper, adding the oil in a steady stream, whisking until the dressing emulsifies. Add the sesame seeds and the garlic.
Spoon the dressing over the leeks and sprinkle with parsley.
Serves 4-8

CHILLED CURRIED LEEK SOUP

3 leeks, white part only, sliced
1½ oz/40 g butter
3 ripe tomatoes, peeled and chopped
¼ teaspoon curry powder, or more to taste
½ pint/300 ml chicken stock
½ pint/300 ml milk
salt to taste
pinch of sugar
1 (5 fl oz/142 ml) carton single cream
fresh chives, chopped

In a heavy saucepan melt the butter. Add the sliced leeks and cook, uncovered, over moderate heat until soft.
Add the tomatoes, curry and stock. Continue cooking for at least 10 more minutes.
Cool and place the mixture in an electric blender or mixer.
Slowly add the milk and sugar. Blend until smooth; strain the mixture through a sieve afterwards. Blend in the cream and chill the soup, covered, for several hours.
Just before serving correct the seasoning.
Serve very cold in chilled soup plates or bowls. Sprinkle with chopped chives.
Serves 4-6

COLD VICHYSSOISE

2 leeks, white parts only, chopped
1 oz/25 g unsalted butter
1 onion, chopped
1¾ pints/1 litre chicken stock
5 large potatoes, peeled and sliced
1 bay leaf
¼ teaspoon ground white pepper
pinch of cayenne pepper
1 (5 fl oz/142 ml) carton single cream
fresh chives, chopped
paprika

In a heavy saucepan melt the butter. Add the leeks and the onion. Sauté over low heat until the vegetables begin to soften.

Add the stock, potatoes, bay leaf, white pepper and cayenne. Bring to boil uncovered. Reduce the heat and simmer for 35-40 minutes, covered.

Cool, then blend the mixture in a blender or mixer until smooth.

Place the soup, covered, in the refrigerator for 4 hours or more.

Just before serving correct the seasoning and stir in the cream.

Serve in chilled soup bowls or plates. Garnish with chopped chives and dust with paprika.

Serves 4-6

PLAIN LEEK SOUP

3-4 leeks, white parts only
1½ oz/40 g butter
2½ pints/1.5 litres hot water
1 lb/450 g potatoes, peeled and sliced
1 teaspoon salt
¼ teaspoon nutmeg, freshly ground
freshly ground black pepper
1 (5 fl oz/142 g) carton single cream

Shred the white parts of the leeks and wash them thoroughly.

In a heavy saucepan melt the butter and gently sauté the leeks until they begin to soften.

Add the water, sliced potatoes, nutmeg, pepper and salt. Cook over moderate heat for 35 minutes or until vegetables are soft.

Just before serving, add the cream and pour the hot soup into warmed plates or bowls.

Serves 4-6

Mushrooms

About 400BC Hippocrates referred in his writings to the popularity of mushrooms. Julius Caesar described mushrooms as 'food for the gods'. But mushrooms have been as much feared as enjoyed. Of the 38,000 known varieties there are a number of fatally poisonous or hallucinogenic kinds: Roman emperors Tiberius and Claudius were victims of mushroom poisoning as well as Pope Clement VIII and Charles V of France.

Mushrooms have been known to the Chinese and Japanese cuisine for a very long time. In Europe mushrooms were first cultivated in France at the end of the seventeenth century and considered a great delicacy, but in England they only gained wide popularity in the late 1940s.

The mushroom we buy today comes in three different shapes: 'button' mushroom, which is small, crisp and white, 'cup' mushroom, which is medium-sized showing pinkish gills, and the 'flat' mushroom, which is fully opened, mature and much stronger in flavour.

Raw mushrooms contain 2 calories per oz/25 g.

They contain potassium, phosphorus and vitamin B.

Tips

■ Cut off the stem level with the cap, and do not pull the stem out, or the cap will shrink too much in cooking.

■ The button and cup mushrooms only need to be wiped, the flat mushroom has a strong skin and needs to be peeled.

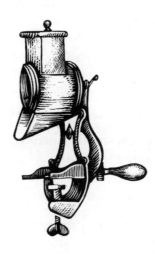

MUSHROOM À LA GRÈCQUE

1 lb/450 g button mushrooms
2 medium onions, finely chopped
4 tablespoons olive oil
2 carrots, sliced
1 clove of garlic, crushed
1 bay leaf
¼ pint/150 ml white wine
salt and freshly ground black pepper
1 tablespoon parsley, finely chopped

In a heavy saucepan fry the onions, garlic and carrot in the oil over moderate heat.
When the vegetables are soft, but not browned, add the bay leaf, wine and salt and pepper to taste. Bring it to the boil, then reduce the heat and simmer the mixture for 1 minute.
Add the mushrooms to the pan. Cover, and cook gently for 5-7 minutes.
Allow to cool, then chill, covered, for at least 4 hours.
Serve very cold in small individual dishes. Sprinkle each portion with chopped parsley.
Serves 4

MARINATED MUSHROOMS

8 oz/225 g button mushrooms, sliced
½ teaspoon powdered English mustard
1 clove of garlic, crushed
¼ pint/150 ml cider vinegar
6-8 drops tabasco sauce
1 bay leaf
fresh chives, or spring onion tops, finely chopped
salt and freshly ground white pepper
crisp lettuce leaves

Put the mushrooms in a glass bowl.
In a separate bowl whisk together the mustard, garlic, vinegar, tabasco, white pepper and salt. Pour the marinade over the mushrooms and add a bay leaf.

Leave the mushrooms to marinate, covered, in a cool place for 8 hours or overnight.

Remove the bay leaf and drain, discarding the marinade.

Serve the mushrooms on individual plates or in bowls, lined with lettuce leaves.

Sprinkle each portion with chives or spring onion tops and serve chilled.

Serves 4

MUSHROOMS IN PORT

1 lb/450 g tiny button mushrooms
3½ oz/100 g butter
1 onion, finely chopped
4 tablespoons ruby port
salt and freshly ground black pepper
4 tablespoons double cream
4-6 slices white bread
fresh parsley, chopped

Wipe the mushrooms, discarding the stalks.

Melt half of the butter in a frying-pan. Add the onion and fry until transparent but not browned. Add the mushrooms and continue to cook over low heat for about 3 minutes.

Pour in the port and add salt and pepper to taste. Stir, then simmer for 3-5 minutes. Slowly add the cream and heat through.

In a separate frying-pan fry the slices of bread in the remaining butter.

Serve the mushrooms very hot on the fried bread slices. Sprinkle with parsley.

Serve immediately.

Serves 4-6

MUSHROOMS WITH BRANDY

6 oz/175 g button or cup mushrooms
1 onion, finely chopped
1 clove of garlic, crushed
2 oz/50 g butter
3 tablespoons brandy
salt and freshly ground black pepper

Wipe and halve the mushrooms, discarding the stalks.
Fry the onion with the garlic in the butter until the onion is golden. Add the halved mushrooms, the salt and pepper. Cover the saucepan and cook gently over low heat for about 5 minutes. Add the brandy, heat through, then put a lighted match to the surface of the mixture to set alight. Let the flames die down and serve immediately on warmed plates.
Serves 4

HOT MUSHROOMS WITH PAPRIKA

1 lb/450 g small button mushrooms
1 oz/25 g butter
1¼ teaspoons sweet paprika
pinch of cayenne pepper
salt and coarsely ground white pepper
¼ pint/150 ml sour cream
2 teaspoons fresh dill, finely chopped, OR
½ teaspoon dried dill

Wipe the mushrooms, discarding the stalks.
Melt the butter in a heavy saucepan and add the mushrooms. Stir and add the paprika, cayenne, salt and pepper. Simmer over very low heat for about 5 minutes.
Stir in the sour cream and the dill. Heat through but do not boil.
Serve immediately.
Serves 4

MUSHROOMS IN SOUR CREAM

1 lb/450 g button mushrooms
4 spring onions, sliced thinly
4 oz/100 g butter
1 oz/25 g flour
¼ pint/150 ml sour cream
salt and freshly ground black pepper
cayenne pepper
4-6 rounds of buttered toast

Wipe and slice the mushrooms, discarding the stalks.

Sauté the mushrooms together with the spring onions in 2 oz/50 g of the butter over moderate heat, stirring from time to time. Cook for about 10 minutes, or until the mushrooms have given off their liquid. Set aside.

In a heavy saucepan melt the remaining 2 oz/50 g of the butter and over low heat stir in the flour. Blend it into a thick, smooth paste and gradually stir in the liquid from the mushroom mixture. Stir, then add the mushrooms, the spring onions and all their liquid. Season with salt, pepper and cayenne pepper to taste.

Stir in the sour cream, heating the mixture through, without boiling.

Serve hot on hot buttered rounds of toast.

Serves 4-6

183

MUSHROOMS IN MUSTARD SAUCE

1 lb/450 g button mushrooms
¼ pint/150 ml olive oil
juice of 1 lemon
10 black peppercorns
2 bay leaves
1 tablespoon Dijon mustard
salt
2 tablespoons parsley, finely chopped

Wipe and slice the mushrooms, discarding the stalks.
Place the mushrooms in a glass bowl.
In a separate bowl blend the oil, lemon juice, peppercorns and bay leaves. Pour the marinade over the mushrooms and marinate them for at least 1 day, tossing gently from time to time.
Drain, and discard the peppercorns and the bay leaves. Combine the juices from the mushrooms with the mustard. Add a little more oil and lemon juice if there is not enough liquid left. Blend very well and correct the seasoning.
Drizzle the sauce over the mushrooms, sprinkle with parsley and serve very cold on chilled plates.
Serves 4-6

MUSHROOM COCKTAIL

This simple recipe makes a popular and delicious starter to any meal.

½ round lettuce, washed, dried and shredded
12 oz/350 g button mushrooms
¼ pint/150 ml double cream
2 tablespoons mayonnaise, see page 266
2 tablespoons tomato ketchup
1 tablespoon lemon juice
salt and freshly ground black pepper
fresh parsley, finely chopped
paprika

Shred the lettuce and fill the bottom of 4 salad bowls or cocktail glasses. Set aside.

Wipe the mushrooms, remove the stalks and cover the mushrooms with boiling water. Leave for 2 minutes, drain and slice them thinly.

In a bowl combine the cream, mayonnaise, tomato ketchup, lemon juice, salt and pepper. Add the mushrooms and blend well.

Spoon the mixture onto the shredded lettuce.

Sprinkle each portion with parsley and dust with paprika. Serve very cold.

Serves 4

MUSHROOM AND PRAWN COCKTAIL

6 oz/175 g button mushrooms
6 oz/175 g prawns, cooked and peeled
½ lettuce, washed, dried and shredded

for the dressing
4 tablespoons vegetable oil
2 tablespoons olive oil
1 tablespoon white wine vinegar
1 clove of garlic, crushed
1 tablespoon fresh mint, finely chopped
1 teaspoon fresh parsley, finely chopped
salt and freshly ground black pepper
pinch of cayenne pepper

Wipe and slice the mushrooms, discarding the stalks.

Blend all the ingredients for the dressing in an electric blender or mixer.

Pour the dressing into a bowl and add the mushrooms and prawns. Cover and chill for at least 6 hours.

Serve very cold in individual small dishes or cocktail glasses lined with lettuce.

Serves 4

MUSHROOM AND CARROT PÂTÉ

A marvellous party dish for more than eight people.

1 large onion, chopped
2 oz/50 g butter
2 cloves of garlic, crushed
1 lb/450 g mushrooms, chopped
1¼ lb/575 g carrots, chopped
4 large eggs, lightly beaten
4 oz/100 g ground blanched almonds
2 oz/50 g Parmesan cheese, grated
2 oz/50 g Gruyère cheese, grated
1 oz/25 g parsley, finely chopped
1 teaspoon dried thyme
½ teaspoon dried sage
½ teaspoon dried marjoram
lemon juice to taste
1 bay leaf
sour cream
2 teaspoons fresh dill, chopped, OR
1 teaspoon dried dill
salt and freshly ground black pepper

In a heavy saucepan cook the onion and the garlic in the butter over moderate heat, stirring, until the vegetables are softened. Add the mushrooms and salt and pepper to taste. Cook, stirring frequently, until almost all the mushroom liquid is evaporated. Blend the mixture in an electric blender or mixer until smooth.

Transfer it to a large bowl and add the carrots, eggs, almonds, Parmesan, Gruyère, parsley, thyme, sage, marjoram, lemon juice and salt and pepper to taste. Combine well.

Spoon the mixture into a lightly buttered meat-loaf tin, or into a similar shaped ovenproof dish. Put the bay leaf in the centre and cover it with a triple layer of buttered tinfoil.

Set the tin in a roasting dish with enough water to reach two-thirds up the sides of the meat-loaf tin. Bake in the middle of a preheated oven (350°F/180°C/Gas Mark 4) for 1 hour 30 minutes, or until a skewer inserted in the middle comes out clean. Transfer the tin to a rack, let the pâté cool, then chill it overnight.

Slice the pâté and serve it with a separate bowl of sour cream mixed with dill. Serve cold with hot toast, or brown bread.
Serves 8-10

PORTUGUESE MUSHROOMS

12 large mushrooms
1 (4½ oz/120 g) tin sardines in oil
2 tablespoons spring onions, chopped
1 oz/25 g toasted breadcrumbs
2 tablespoons mayonnaise, see page 266
juice of 1 lemon
rind of 1 lemon, finely grated
dash of tabasco sauce
salt and freshly ground black pepper
crisp cold lettuce leaves
finely chopped parsley

Wash the mushrooms and wipe them dry. Chop the stalks.
Empty the sardines with the oil into a bowl. Remove the backbones and tails of the fish and mash flesh. Add the spring onions, breadcrumbs, chopped mushroom stalks, mayonnaise, lemon juice and rind, tabasco sauce and salt and pepper.
Blend the mixture well and spoon it into the mushroom caps.
Sprinkle with chopped parsley and serve cold on a bed of lettuce leaves.
Serves 4

MUSHROOM MALAGA

1 lb/450 g small button mushrooms
3 tablespoons water
3 tablespoons olive oil
4 tablespoons white wine
1½ tablespoons lemon juice
a sprig of parsley
1½ tablespoons tomato purée
salt and freshly ground pepper
chopped parsley

Wipe the mushrooms, discarding the stalks.
In a saucepan combine the water, oil, wine, lemon juice and a sprig of parsley. Bring to boil, then simmer for 5 minutes.
Add the tomato purée, mushrooms, salt and pepper and cook over low heat for another 5-8 minutes.
Leave to cool, then chill for at least 2 hours.
Sprinkle with parsley. Serve very cold.
Serves 4-6

POTTED MUSHROOMS

6 oz/175 g button or cup mushrooms
1 clove of garlic, crushed
6 oz/175 g butter
grated rind of 1 lemon
few drops of Worcestershire sauce
salt and freshly ground white pepper

Wipe the mushrooms, discarding the stalks. Coarsely chop the mushrooms.
Fry the garlic in half of the butter for 1 minute. Add the mushrooms and continue frying over moderate heat for a further 3 minutes.
Drain the mushrooms in a sieve, then place in 4 individual dishes.
Combine the remaining butter, the grated lemon rind, Worcestershire sauce, salt and pepper and heat until the butter has melted.

Pour it over the mushrooms and cool, then chill for several hours.

Serve cold with thin slices of hot buttered toast.

Serves 4

DEEP FRIED MUSHROOMS

1 lb/450 g button mushrooms
6 oz/175 g plain flour
seasoned flour
2 eggs, lightly beaten
½ pint/300 ml milk
1 clove of garlic, crushed
oil for deep frying
salt and freshly ground black pepper
tartar sauce, see page 272

Wipe the mushrooms and discard the stalks. Coat with seasoned flour.

Sieve the plain flour into a bowl, add salt and pepper, the lightly beaten eggs and some of the milk. Mix it into a smooth paste and, gradually, beat in the remaining milk; then add the crushed garlic.

Dip the mushrooms into this mixture, coating them evenly, letting excess drip off.

Carefully drop each mushroom into the hot oil of a deep fryer. Fry until they are crisp and golden. Drain the mushrooms on absorbent kitchen paper.

Serve the mushrooms very hot on warmed plates with tartar sauce.

Serves 4-6

DEEP FRIED MUSHROOMS WITH PÂTÉ

24 cup mushrooms, wiped, stalks discarded
1 large egg
1 teaspoon water
4 oz/100 g stale breadcrumbs
4 fl oz/100 ml dry red wine
16 fl oz/450 ml brown gravy
oil for deep frying

for the pâté
1 small onion, very finely chopped
1 oz/25 g butter
5 oz/150 g chicken livers, trimmed and quartered
1 tablespoon double cream
2 tablespoons fresh parsley, finely chopped
pinch of powdered thyme
salt and pepper

To make the pâté

In a heavy frying-pan sauté the onion in half of the butter over moderate heat until it is soft. Add the chicken livers and cook, increasing heat slightly, for 2-3 minutes, or until the livers are brown on the outside, but still pink within.
Cool for 2 minutes.

In an electric blender or mixer purée the chicken liver mixture with the remaining butter, cream, parsley, thyme, salt and pepper until the mixture is very smooth. Transfer the pâté to a separate bowl and chill, covered, until it is firm.

Mound the pâté firmly in the mushroom caps and smooth the tops with the blade of a knife.
Beat the egg with a teaspoon of water and dip the mushrooms into the egg mixture, letting excess drip off, then dredge the mushrooms with breadcrumbs, shaking off any excess. Put the mushrooms in one layer on a platter and chill for 1 hour.
In a stainless steel or enamel saucepan reduce the wine by half, over moderate heat. Stir in the brown gravy and keep the sauce warm.
Deep fry the mushrooms in the oil in 3 or 4 batches until they are golden brown.
Transfer them with a slotted spoon to absorbent kitchen

paper to drain, and keep warm.

Transfer the sauce to a warm sauce-boat, arrange the mushrooms on a heated platter and serve them hot, accompanied by the sauce.

Serves 4

CREAMED MUSHROOM SOUP

1 lb/450 g veal bones
1 carrot, scraped
½ parsnip, peeled
1 onion, chopped
1 bay leaf
4 black peppercorns
1¾ pints/1 litre water
½ lb/225 g mushrooms, sliced
1 tablespoon parsley, finely chopped
3 egg yolks
6 tablespoons single cream
2 tablespoons butter
1 tablespoon lemon juice
salt to taste

In a large saucepan combine the veal bones, carrot, parsnip, onion, bay leaf, peppercorns and salt. Pour in the water and bring the mixture to boil.

Skim and simmer, covered, for 2 hours.

Sauté the sliced mushrooms and parsley in the butter until tender.

Strain the veal stock and pour it over the mushrooms. Bring it to boil, then simmer for 5 minutes.

Beat the egg yolks with the cream and the lemon juice and blend it into the soup just before serving.

Do not boil the soup again or it will curdle.

Serve hot in warmed soup bowls or soup plates.

Serves 4-6

HAM STUFFED MUSHROOMS

1 lb/450 g large mushrooms
1 medium onion, finely chopped
3 tablespoons fresh parsley, finely chopped
1 oz/25 g butter
3 oz/75 g cooked ham, finely chopped
grated rind of 1 lemon
2 hard-boiled eggs, sieved

for the dressing
2 shallots, finely chopped
2 tablespoons fresh parsley, finely chopped
3 tablespoons tarragon vinegar
1 tablespoon Dijon mustard
6 tablespoons walnut oil
6 tablespoons vegetable oil
1 hard-boiled egg yolk, sieved
2 tablespoons mayonnaise, see page 266
salt and pepper

Wash the mushrooms and wipe them dry. Chop the mushroom stalks.

In a heavy saucepan sauté the onion and the mushroom stalks in the butter over moderately high heat, stirring, for 2 minutes. Remove the pan from the heat and stir in the parsley, ham, lemon rind, eggs, salt and pepper.

Mix well, pile the stuffing in the mushroom caps and arrange the stuffed mushrooms in one layer on a serving dish.

In a small bowl combine the shallots, parsley, vinegar and mustard. Slowly add the walnut oil, whisking, and the vegetable oil. Whisk until the dressing emulsifies.

In a separate bowl blend the egg yolk with the mayonnaise, whisk and fold it into the dressing.

Season the dressing with salt and pepper and serve it in a sauce-boat beside the stuffed mushrooms.

Serve very cold.

Serves 4-6

Onion

The onion, a member of the lily family, is a native of Asia, probably Palestine. One of the oldest known vegetables, it has been cultivated from earliest time.

The Roman poet Martial praised the onion for its aphrodisiac powers: 'If your wife is old and your member is exhausted, eat onions in plenty'.

The onion was worshipped in Egypt and listed in the records of the slaves who built the great pyramids in Giza. A bouquet of onions was placed into a mummy's hand to pass him through the afterworld.

By the beginning of the Christian era, they had become so sacred in Egypt that the priests prohibited the eating of onions.

There are several varieties: larger and milder onions grow in warmer climates, while smaller and more strongly-flavoured onions thrive in cooler regions. Colours vary from white, yellow, light brown to purple red. White onions are usually milder than the red and yellow variety, and are more suitable for making sauces and soups.

The onion contains potassium and vitamins B and C.

1 oz/25 g raw onion contains 7 calories.

ONIONS À LA GRÈCQUE

2 lb/900 g tiny onions
½ pint/300 ml dry white wine
½ pint chicken stock
1 clove of garlic, crushed
juice of 1 lemon
4 tablespoons tomato purée
2 tablespoons white wine vinegar
1 bay leaf
salt and freshly ground black pepper
cayenne pepper
fresh parsley, coarsely chopped
lemon slices

Blanch the onions in boiling water for about 1 minute: drain and peel them. Trim the roots and the stems to prevent them from falling apart during cooking.

In a shallow saucepan combine the onions, wine, stock, garlic, lemon juice, tomato purée, vinegar, bay leaf, salt and plenty of freshly ground black pepper.

Bring to boil, uncovered, reduce the heat and cook for 15 minutes, or until the onions are tender.

With a slotted spoon transfer the onions to a serving dish.

Boil the liquid over high heat until the cooking liquid is reduced to ½ pint/300 ml, or a little less.

Add cayenne pepper, taste for seasoning and discard the bay leaf. Pour the liquid over the onions, cover and chill for 1 day.

Before serving sprinkle the onions with chopped parsley. Serve chilled with slices of lemon.

Serves 4-6

SPANISH ONION SALAD

4 large Spanish onions, peeled
4 oz/100 g black olives, pitted
1 tablespoon fresh parsley, chopped
4 fl oz/100 ml olive oil
2 fl oz/50 ml red wine vinegar
salt and freshly ground black pepper

Cook the onions in boiling salted water for 25 minutes, or until they are tender. Drain thoroughly and slice them very thickly.

Arrange the onion slices on a flat serving dish, sprinkle with the olives, parsley and plenty of freshly ground black pepper. In a separate dish whisk the olive oil with the vinegar until it emulsifies.

Pour it over the onion mixture and serve immediately. Serve warm with French bread.

Serves 4

ONION AND ORANGE SALAD

It is thought that this recipe arrived in France from the Middle East during the late nineteenth century. A refreshing starter to any meal.

4 large onions
3 oranges
4 tablespoons walnut oil
2 tablespoons white wine vinegar
salt and freshly ground black pepper
2 oz/50 g pistachio nuts, chopped

Peel and slice the onions into very thin rings. Blanch in boiling water for 15 seconds, then immediately plunge the onion rings into iced water. Drain and pat dry.

Peel the oranges, cut them into very thin slices, removing any pips and membrane.

In a flat serving dish mix the onion rings with the orange slices.

In a separate bowl whisk the oil with the vinegar until it emulsifies. Add the pepper and salt to taste and pour the dressing over the onion and orange mixture.

Refrigerate, covered, for 30 minutes.

Sprinkle with chopped nuts. Serve very cold.

Serves 4

ONIONS 'MONEGASQUE'

1 carrot, coarsely chopped
1 lb/450 g button onions, peeled
¼ pint/150 ml dry white wine
2 fl oz/50 ml water
1 tablespoon lemon juice
1 bay leaf
2 oz/50 g seedless raisins
2 teaspoons brown sugar
1 clove of garlic, crushed
1 tablespoon tomato purée
2 tablespoons olive oil
salt and freshly ground black pepper
chopped parsley

In a heavy saucepan sauté the carrot in 1½ tablespoons of the oil until soft and slightly golden.

Remove and combine in a separate saucepan with the onions, wine, water, lemon juice, bay leaf, raisins, sugar, garlic, tomato purée, salt and pepper.

Bring to boil, then reduce the heat and simmer over low heat for 1 hour, or until the onions are cooked through and the sauce has reduced a little.

Remove the bay leaf and chill the mixture for several hours, covered.

Just before serving, correct the seasoning, add a little olive oil and sprinkle with chopped parsley.

Serve very cold in 4 individual, chilled salad plates.

Serves 4

FRENCH ONION SOUP

The classic French onion soup is the perfect winter starter.

2 oz/50 g butter
2 tablespoons vegetable oil
2 tablespoons onion, thinly sliced
1 teaspoon salt
3 tablespoons cornflour
generous 2½ pints/1.5 litres beef stock
freshly ground black pepper

for the croûtons
12-16 slices of French bread
3 teaspoons olive oil
1 clove of garlic
4 oz/100 g Parmesan cheese, grated

Melt the butter and the oil in a heavy saucepan. Stir in the onions, add the salt and cook, uncovered, over low heat for 25-30 minutes. Remove the pan from the heat before the onions are browned.

Sprinkle the cornflour over the onions and cook, over low heat, stirring all the time, for 2-3 minutes. Remove the saucepan from the heat.

In a separate saucepan bring the stock to simmer, then stir the hot stock into the onions. Simmer for 30-40 minutes.

Cool and skim off the fat.

Add salt and pepper to taste and reheat. Serve hot with croûtons.

While the soup simmers prepare the *croûtons*.

To make the croûtons
Preheat the oven to 375°F/190°C/Gas Mark 5. Spread the slices of bread on a baking sheet after brushing both sides with a little olive oil. Bake the slices for about 15 minutes on each side, or until completely dry and slightly browned.

Rub each side with the cut clove of garlic and set aside.

Place the *croûtons* in a large soup terrine, or individual soup dishes, and ladle the hot soup over them.

Serve the cheese separately.

Serves 6-8

WHITE ONION SOUP WITH MILK

6 medium onions, sliced thickly
1 oz/25 g butter
½ pint/300 ml boiling water
1¾ pints/1 litre milk
1 tablespoon plain flour
salt to taste
freshly ground white pepper
1 tablespoon single cream

Melt the butter and add the onions. Cook over high heat for 3 minutes. Add the flour and stir, adding the water gradually. Reduce the heat, season with salt and white pepper and cook over medium heat for 10 minutes. Stir again and slowly add the milk. Simmer gently, covered, for 15-20 minutes, or until the onions are very soft.

Correct the seasoning and add a tablespoon of single cream just before serving.

Serves 6

Oyster

The oyster, an edible bivalve shellfish, has been considered a delicacy for centuries.

Ancient shell heaps found in America point to the probability that the Indians ate oysters long before the first European settlers arrived on the continent.

The oyster was considered a great delicacy in ancient Greece, and the oyster shell was used as ballot paper on which the voter scratched his choice with a sharp tool.

No good dinner in ancient Rome was complete without its course of oysters. The preferred variety came from the shores of occupied Britain. At great expense, packed in snow and ice, oysters were imported for the Imperial capital's banquets and feasts.

Today there is a multitude of oysters to choose from, although they are becoming more and more expensive.

Oysters are highly nutritive food and they are, contrary to other shellfish, easily digestible.

Oysters contain phosphorus, calcium, iodine, iron and vitamin B.
6 oysters contain 60 calories.

Tips

■ Normally, although not always, the shells of dead oysters are a little open, while the shells of live oysters are tightly closed. If tapping the shell produces a hollow sound, the oyster is more than likely dead. Always discard suspect oysters.

■ It is important to eat oysters very fresh, and they ought always to be bought in their shells.

● Raw oysters should be eaten as soon as possible after opening, as exposure to air will spoil their flavour.

■ In England, oysters are in season from September to April.

To Open and Prepare Oysters

Use the oysters immediately after opening and discard any oysters which do not close when handled.

Wash the oysters in their shells. Hold the thick part in the palm of your hand and with a thin sharp knife prise between the shells near the back; then run a knife along to cut the muscle which holds the shells together. *See illustration.*

Place the oysters in a strainer over a bowl, so that any liquor may be saved and used for sauces.

Inspect each oyster very carefully. Cloudy oysters are not fit to eat.

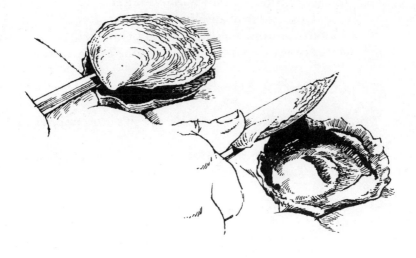

RAW OYSTERS

12 oysters, opened, but left on the lower shell
crushed ice
lemon halves

Serve the oysters in their lower shells together with the lemon halves on a bed of crushed ice. Eat immediately.
Serves 2

OYSTERS WITH SHERRY SAUCE

12 oysters, opened, but left on the lower shell
¼ pint/150 ml wine vinegar
1 tablespoon medium dry sherry
2 tablespoons shallots, finely chopped
1½ teaspoons coarsely ground black pepper
salt
crushed ice

In a bowl combine the vinegar, sherry, shallots, pepper and salt to taste.
Arrange the oysters on a platter covered with crushed ice.
Serve the sauce separately in a sauce-boat.
Serves 2

OYSTERS IN CHAMPAGNE

24 oysters, opened
½ pint/300 ml champagne
½ pint/300 ml chicken consommé
2 oz/50 g butter
salt and freshly ground white pepper

Pour the champagne and the consommé into a chafting dish and bring to boiling point.
Immediately add the liquid from the oysters and bring to boil again.
Add the oysters and extinguish the flame under the chafting dish.
Add the butter, salt and pepper to taste.
Serve immediately.
Serves 4

OYSTERS IN SCALLOP SHELLS

12 oysters, removed from shells and liquor reserved
2 tablespoons water
juice of 1 lemon
2 oz/50 g butter
1 oz/25 g flour
2 tablespoons dry white wine
pinch of nutmeg
salt and freshly ground white pepper
2 egg yolks
¼ pint/150 ml single cream
1 oz/25 g Parmesan cheese, grated
1 oz/25 g toasted breadcrumbs

Put the oysters into a saucepan over low heat with the water and all the liquid from the oysters until they are well heated through.

Remove the oysters from the heat and add the lemon juice. Drain the oysters well and remove the beards. Reserve the oyster gravy.

Melt the butter in a heavy saucepan and stir in the flour. Slowly add the oyster gravy, stirring, and the white wine. Stir over low heat until the sauce begins to thicken. Season with nutmeg, salt and pepper.

Lightly beat the egg yolks together with the cream and stir into the sauce at the last minute. Add the oysters, stirring well.

Pour this mixture into lightly buttered scallop dishes, sprinkle the top with Parmesan and breadcrumbs.

Bake in a moderately hot oven at 350°F/180°C/Gas Mark 4 for 10-15 minutes, or until the tops are light and golden.

Serve immediately.

Serves 4

OYSTER COCKTAIL

24 oysters, opened, but left on the lower shell
1 teaspoon grated horseradish
4 tablespoons lemon juice
4 tablespoons tomato ketchup
dash of tabasco sauce
½ teaspoon salt
1 tablespoon white wine vinegar
crushed ice

In a bowl mix the horseradish with the lemon juice, ketchup, tabasco, salt and vinegar. Chill, covered, for at least 1 hour.
Serve the oysters, in their half shells, on a platter covered with crushed ice.
Serve the well-chilled sauce separately.
Serves 4

FRIED OYSTERS

24 oysters, shelled and drained
scant ¼ pint/125 ml milk
1 large egg, beaten
1 tablespoon Worcestershire sauce
8 oz/225 g stale breadcrumbs
oil for deep frying
lemon wedges,
tartar sauce, see page 272

In a shallow bowl whisk together the milk, egg and Worcestershire sauce. Add the oysters and let them stand, covered, for 20 minutes.
Roll the oyster in the breadcrumbs, coating them well. Arrange them in one layer on a large plate and chill, covered loosely, for 30 minutes.
In a deep frying-pan heat the oil and fry the oysters in batches, 45 seconds on each side, or until they are golden.
With a slotted spoon transfer them to a heated platter.
Garnish with lemon wedges and serve tartar sauce separately.
Serves 4

OYSTERS ROCKEFELLER

24 oysters, opened, but left on the lower shell
6 shallots, finely chopped
2 oz/50 g butter
4 tablespoons stale breadcrumbs
1 bunch watercress, stalks discarded, leaves chopped
2 tablespoons parsley, chopped
1 stalk celery, chopped
¼ teaspoon dried tarragon
¼ teaspoon dried chervil
dash of tabasco sauce
salt
cayenne pepper
4 tablespoons Pernod
rock salt

Sauté the shallots in half of the butter until they are transparent. Sprinkle in the breadcrumbs and stir over low heat until they are slightly browned.

Mix the watercress leaves with the parsley and the celery.

Combine the shallots and breadcrumb mixture with the chopped greens in a large bowl. Add the tarragon, chervil, tabasco, salt and cayenne pepper. Mix well, then slowly add the Pernod. Blend well and add the remaining butter.

Pound the mixture into a smooth, thickish paste.

Place a layer of rock salt in a baking tin large enough to hold the oysters in one layer. Place the oysters on the salt. Place 1 tablespoon of the green herb butter on each oyster.

Bake the oysters in a hot oven (425°F/220°C/Gas Mark 7) for 4-5 minutes, or until the edges begin to curl and the butter has melted.

Serve immediately.

Serves 4

OYSTERS EN BROCHETTE

12 oysters, shelled and drained
4 slices lean bacon
6 fl oz/175 ml evaporated milk
about 2 oz/50 g breadcrumbs
6 oz/50 g flour, seasoned with salt and pepper
4 slices of toast
4 lemon wedges

Grill the bacon until the fat on the bacon is translucent but not golden. With a slotted spoon transfer the bacon to absorbent kitchen paper to drain, cool and cut into 1 inch/ 2.5 cm pieces. On each of the four 8 inch/30 cm skewers thread 4 pieces of bacon alternately with 3 of the oysters, skewering each oyster twice to achieve a plump shape.

In two separate dishes have ready the milk and the breadcrumbs. Dip the brochette in the milk, letting any excess drip off, then dredge with flour, shaking off the excess.

Deep fry the brochettes, 2 batches at a time, for about 2 minutes, or until golden brown. Transfer them with a slotted spoon to absorbent kitchen paper to drain.

Arrange each brochette on a slice of toast set on a small hot serving plate.

Serve with lemon wedges.

Serves 4

POACHED OYSTERS WITH LEEK AND CREAM SAUCE

12 oysters, shelled, liquor and shells reserved
1 leek, white part only
1 shallot
1 oz/25 g butter
½ pint/300 ml champagne
8 fl oz/250 ml double cream
1 tablespoon lemon juice
salt
cayenne pepper and white pepper

Cut the white part of the leek into fine *julienne* strips and blanch them in a saucepan of boiling salted water for 1 minute. Drain the leek strips well.

In a heavy saucepan cook the shallot in the butter over moderate heat, stirring, until it is translucent. Add the champagne and reduce the liquid to two.thirds over moderately high heat. Stir in the oyster liquor, salt, cayenne pepper and add the oysters. Poach them over moderately low heat until the edges begin to curl.

With a slotted spoon transfer the oysters to the reserved shells and keep them warm.

Reduce the poaching liquid by half and add the cream. Reduce the sauce until it is thickened and season with lemon juice, salt and white pepper. Divide the oysters in their shells between 2 serving plates and arrange 1 tablespoon of the leek on top of each oyster. Top the oysters with the sauce and serve hot.

Serves 2

OYSTERS CASINO

24 oysters, opened and left on the lower shell
4 slices streaky bacon, each cut into 4-6 pieces
3 oz/75 g butter
3 shallots, finely chopped
1 red pepper, seeded and finely chopped
3 tablespoons parsley, finely chopped
2 teaspoons lemon juice
rock salt

In a heavy pan cook the bacon over moderate heat, stirring, until it is golden. With a slotted spoon transfer it to absorbent kitchen paper to drain.

Combine the butter, shallots, red pepper, parsley and lemon juice in a bowl. Spread the rock salt ½ inch/1 cm deep in a baking dish large enough to hold the oysters in one layer.

Heat the dish in a preheated very hot oven (450°F/230°C/ Gas Mark 8) for 5 minutes. Arrange the oysters on the salt, pressing the shells slightly into the salt to steady them. Divide the butter mixture among the oysters and top each oyster with a piece of bacon.

Bake the oysters in the hot oven for 5 minutes, or until the bacon is crisp.

Serve hot.

Serves 4-6

If you like snails, *Snails in Herb Butter* (see page 238) is the classic recipe.

The subtle flavour of strawberries and the delicate taste of turkey make *Turkey and Strawberry Cocktail* a unique starter. (See page 232).

Above right: *Smoked Chicken and Blue Cheese Salad*: an exotic, tangy and unusual starter. (See page 229).

Below right: the versatile tomato lends itself to a variety of appetizing starters: *Bel's Quick Tomato Starter*, top left (see page 248), *Tomato Gervais*, top right (see page 253), *Tomato Rose*, bottom left (see page 248) and *Accordion Tomato* (see page 249).

A reliable starter, pâté can be prepared well ahead: *Hasty Pâté,* top (see page 225); *Mushroom and Carrot Pâté* (see page 186) and *Scampi Pâté* in ramekins (see page 155).

Pancake

The pancake has been enjoyed around the world for centuries. England has her 'Shrove Tuesday', when, in order to use up all the milk, the butter and the eggs – once forbidden food during the Lent fast – it became, at first custom, and then tradition to eat pancakes.

The pancake is also part of the American heritage. To the early settler acorn or beechnut pancakes were a whole meal, but now the pancake is mainly an American breakfast habit. In Russia 'blinis' are served as appetizers, often topped with caviar and sour cream. The French have their fabled 'crêpes Suzette', the Mexicans their 'tortillas' and the Germans their 'Eierkuchen'. In Sweden exquisitely light pancakes with lingonberries are served for dessert, and in China no meal is complete without the crisp fried egg roll.

Successful with every conceivable kind of sauce or filling, pancakes are easy to make and inexpensive if you don't serve 'blinis' with real caviar. Pancakes can be made in advance; they can be stored and they can be frozen.

Tips

■ Never use water after cooking if you want to keep your pan in prime condition. Simply wipe it with a buttered piece of paper kitchen towel and it will never stick.

■ If you want to keep the pancakes warm for several hours, pile them on a heatproof plate, cover them with a large heatproof dish, and when you want to reheat them, put them in a preheated oven (400°F/200°C/Gas Mark 6) for 10 minutes.

■ Pancakes can be stored in the refrigerator for a few days, covered with foil or cling-film. For longer storage, wrap them in foil, 4-6 in a pack, and freeze. Later they must be thawed at room temperature to be easily separated.

BASIC PANCAKE RECIPE FOR SIX PEOPLE

2 oz/50 g plain flour
pinch of salt
1 whole egg plus 1 extra egg yolk
2 tablespoons milk
1-2 tablespoons cold water (or more)
1 tablespoon melted butter

Sift the flour and salt into a mixing bowl. Mix in the egg and the extra egg yolk and beat with a wire whisk.

Add the milk and 1 tablespoon of water.

Melt the butter and blend it into the paste. The mixture should be like thin cream.

Leave it to stand in a cool place for at least 1 hour.

Stir well and if it is too thick, add a further 2-3 tablespoons of cold water.

Use a small omelette or crêpe pan, which you keep exclusively for this type of cooking.

Heat it over medium temperature. Wipe round with a piece of buttered kitchen paper.

Pour a large tablespoon of the batter into the pan, rotating, so that the mixture spreads evenly over the bottom without being too thick.

When the top surface loses its wet appearance and the pancake browns underneath, carefully turn it over and lightly brown it on the other side.

Slide the pancake onto a plate and keep warm while you make the rest of the pancakes.

Alternatively the pancake mixture can be prepared in an electric blender or mixer.

Place the milk, egg, extra egg yolk and water into the blender. Switch to slow speed and, gradually, add the flour, the salt and lastly, the melted butter.

Blend for 1 minute. Be careful not to let the mixture become too bubbly.

SEAFOOD PANCAKES

8-12 pancakes, see basic pancake recipe, page 211
4 oz/100 g butter
2 teaspoons curry powder
9 oz/250 g white fish fillets, diced
4 oz/100 g scallops, cleaned and cut in half
4 oz/100 g prawns or shrimps, cooked and shelled
1 tablespoon white flour
4 fl oz/100 ml dry white wine
¼ pint/150 ml chicken stock
2 fl oz/50 ml sour cream
salt and pepper to taste

Melt the butter in a large pan and add the curry powder. Stir for 30 seconds, then add the fish, scallops and prawns or shrimps. Cook for 1 minute over moderately high heat.
Sprinkle the flour over it, and quickly stir to mix.
Add the wine, let it bubble briefly, then add the chicken stock.
Cook for 30 seconds, stirring, and add salt and pepper.
Reduce the heat and add the cream, stirring all the time.
Remove the pan from the heat.
Butter an ovenproof dish large enough to hold the rolled pancakes in one layer. Fill each pancake with about 1 tablespoon of the mixture, using a slotted spoon. Roll up each filled pancake and place them, side by side, on the dish.
Pour over any remaining sauce and warm them through in a preheated oven (350°F/180°C/Gas Mark 4) for about 20 minutes.
Serve hot.
Serves 4-6

SMOKED HADDOCK PANCAKES

8 pancakes, see basic pancake recipe, page 211
12 oz/350 g smoked haddock
1 small red pepper, cored and seeded
1 small green pepper, cored and seeded
1 oz/25 g butter
1 oz/25 g plain flour
¼ pint/150 ml milk
grated nutmeg
pinch of cayenne pepper
freshly ground white pepper
few drops of Worcestershire sauce

Place the haddock in a saucepan and cover with water. Bring to boil and simmer for 5 minutes. Drain the haddock in a colander, reserving ¼ pint/150 ml of the liquid.
Remove the skin and all bones, and flake the fish.
Slice a few rings from the red pepper and reserve. Chop the remaining peppers very finely and mix with the haddock.
In a heavy saucepan melt the butter, stir in the flour and cook, stirring constantly, for 1 minute. Whisk in the haddock liquid and the milk, stirring, until the sauce thickens. Add the nutmeg, cayenne, Worcestershire sauce and white pepper.
Cook over moderate heat for a further 1 minute, stirring all the time. Remove the sauce from the heat and mix three-quarters of it with the fish.
Preheat the oven to 400°F/200°C/Gas Mark 6. Butter an ovenproof dish large enough to hold the rolled pancakes in one layer.
Divide the haddock mixture between the pancakes. Roll up each filled pancake and place them, side by side, on the dish.
Pour the remaining sauce over the pancakes and arrange red pepper rings on top. Cook in the oven for 10-15 minutes.
Serve hot.
Serves 4

RUSSIAN PANCAKES

8-12 pancakes, see basic pancake recipe, page 211
1 (5 fl oz/142 ml) carton cottage cheese
½ onion, finely chopped
small jar of caviar, or mock caviar (lump fish)
sour cream
salt and freshly ground black pepper

Mix the onion with the cottage cheese and season with salt and pepper. Fill each pancake with this mixture and roll it up. Arrange the pancakes on separate plates.
Spread some sour cream across each rolled-up pancake and run a line of caviar across the top.
Serve at room temperature.
Serves 4-6

PANCAKES WITH SPINACH FILLING

8-12 pancakes, see basic recipe, page 211
2 oz/50 g butter
grated nutmeg
1 oz/25 g flour
¼ pint/150 ml hot milk
4 oz/100 g Gruyère cheese
8 oz/225 g cooked spinach, fresh or frozen
salt and freshly ground black pepper

Press all the liquid from the spinach, chop finely and cook over medium heat in half of the butter until the spinach is dry. Add the seasoning and nutmeg.
In a separate pan melt the remaining butter, sprinkle in the flour, add the hot milk and cook until the sauce thickens, stirring briskly all the time. Add the spinach and simmer over low heat for about 5 minutes. Remove the pan from the heat and beat in two-thirds of the cheese.
Put a tablespoon of the mixture in each pancake, roll it up and arrange it in a buttered ovenproof dish large enough to hold the pancakes in one layer. Cover with the remaining sauce and sprinkle with the remaining cheese. Reheat and brown under a hot grill. Serve hot.
Serves 4-6

PANCAKES ITALIA

8-12 pancakes, see basic pancake recipe, page 211
8 oz/225 g Mozzarella cheese
4 thin slices Prosciutto ham
2 oz/50 g butter
1½ oz/40 g flour
½ pint/300 ml hot milk
salt
cayenne pepper
pinch of nutmeg
½ teaspoon dried oregano
½ pint/300 ml double cream
2 egg yolks, lightly beaten
¼ pint/150 ml tomato sauce, see page 271

Cut 8-12 thin strips or slices off the cheese and set aside. Dice the remaining cheese and the Prosciutto.

In a heavy pan melt the butter, stir in the flour and work into a smooth paste, stirring constantly. Slowly add the hot milk, stir until the sauce thickens, then season with salt, cayenne, nutmeg and oregano. Set aside.

In a separate saucepan combine the cream and the beaten egg yolks. Add some of the sauce and whisk until smooth. Return the egg and cream mixture to the first saucepan and add the diced cheese and Prosciutto. Cook over low heat, stirring all the time, until the sauce is thick and golden. Do not let the sauce boil after adding the eggs, or it will curdle.

Butter an ovenproof dish large enough to hold the rolled pancakes in one layer. Coat each pancake with tomato sauce and then with a generous helping of the cheese and Prosciutto sauce. Roll the pancakes and arrange them on the dish. Chill until 1 hour before cooking.

About half an hour before serving time, spoon a little tomato sauce over each rolled-up pancake and top it with a thin slice or strips of Mozzarella cheese. Bake for 20 minutes in a slow oven at 325°F/160°C/Gas Mark 3.

Serve hot.

Serves 4-6

SOUR CREAM AND BACON PANCAKES WITH MELON

8 pancakes, see basic pancake recipe, page 211
8 oz/225 g streaky bacon
1 melon
½ pint/300 ml sour cream
1 clove of garlic, crushed
1 tablespoon fresh dill, chopped, OR
1 teaspoon dried dill weed
salt and freshly ground black pepper
4 oz/100 g Cheddar cheese, freshly grated

Grill or fry the bacon until crisp. Drain it on absorbent kitchen paper and, when cool enough to handle, crumble it.

Halve the melon, scoop out all the seeds and scoop out the flesh with a melon ball cutter. Set aside.

In a bowl combine the bacon, sour cream, dill and garlic. Season with salt and pepper. Mix well, and divide the mixture between the pancakes.

Roll them up and arrange in an ovenproof dish large enough to hold the pancakes in one layer.

Sprinkle the pancakes with grated cheese, cover with foil and place them in a preheated moderately hot oven (375°F/ 190°C/Gas Mark 5) for 20 minutes.

Just before serving, garnish the pancakes with the melon balls.

Serve the pancakes hot.

Serves 4

Pâté

Through centuries the French have perfected the making of pâté to a fine art. In the late fourteenth century for example, they made pâtés of all kinds of meats – even porcupines and badgers could end up in pâtés.

Later, in the seventeenth century, giblets were the main ingredient of heavily peppered pâtés which became a standard lower-class French delicacy.

Today, every restaurant and every charcuterie in France boasts its own *Pâté de Maison*.

In principle, the word 'pâté' should only apply to meat dishes enclosed in pastry. However, it is now used to describe any preparation of finely ground meats, liver etc., put in a pie dish and baked in the oven. The correct term for this type of dish is 'terrine'.

Pâtés are high in calories.

CHICKEN LIVER PÂTÉ

8 oz/225 g chicken livers, chopped
4 oz/100 g butter
1 shallot, finely chopped
1 clove of garlic, crushed
1 medium glass of sherry
pinch of allspice
½ teaspoon powdered English mustard
salt and freshly ground pepper
1 egg

In a heavy covered saucepan sauté the shallot in 2 oz/50 g of the butter over very low heat until it turns transparent.
Add the livers together with the garlic and the remaining butter. Cook gently, stirring from time to time. When they are cooked, the livers must be pale pink inside, or they become too hard and too dry.
Add the sherry, allspice, mustard, salt and plenty of freshly ground black pepper. Simmer for one more minute. Take it off the heat and add the lightly beaten egg.
Place the mixture into an electric blender or mixer and blend at maximum speed until it is very smooth.
Put the mixture into an ovenproof dish, cover it with greaseproof paper and tinfoil and stand it in a roasting dish two-thirds filled with water. Cook at 350°F/180°C/Gas Mark 4 for 1 hour. Cool under a heavy weight overnight.
Melt a little butter and pour it over the pâté to seal it.
Serve with triangles of toast.
Serves 4-6

ITALIAN CHICKEN LIVER PÂTÉ

1 lb/450 g chicken livers, chopped
1 medium onion, chopped
2 oz/50 g butter
2 oz/50 g tinned anchovy fillets, drained
1 tablespoon capers, drained
1 teaspoon brandy
1 teaspoon Marsala
salt and freshly ground black pepper

3222

Sauté the onion in the butter over moderate heat until the onions are transparent. Add the chicken livers, sauté them over moderate heat, stirring, for 2-3 minutes, or until they are browned on the outside but still pink within.

In an electric blender or mixer purée the chicken liver mixture in batches, together with the coarsely chopped anchovies and the capers. Blend until very smooth, then add the brandy, Marsala, salt and plenty of freshly ground black pepper. Blend for a further few seconds.

Transfer the mixture to an earthenware dish and chill, covered, for a few hours. Serve with triangles of hot toast.

Serves 4-6

CHICKEN LIVER AND OLIVE PÂTÉ

1 lb/450 g chicken livers, chopped
1 medium onion, finely chopped
6 oz/175 g butter
1 teaspoon dried *fines herbes*
1 clove of garlic, crushed
1 tablespoon brandy
3 oz/75 g black olives, pitted and chopped
salt and freshly ground black pepper
1 oz/25 g melted butter

Sauté the onion in the butter over moderate heat for 5 minutes, or until the onion is transparent. Add the chicken livers, stir, then add the *fines herbes* and garlic and cook over moderately high heat, stirring, for 5 minutes, or until the livers are browned on the outside but still pink within.

In an electric blender or mixer purée the mixture in batches for about 30 seonds. Scrape down the sides of the bowl of the blender with a wooden or plastic spatula, add the brandy, salt and pepper, and blend for a further 30 seconds.

Transfer the mixture to a bowl, stir in the chopped olives, mix well and pour the mixture into an earthenware dish.

Cover it with greaseproof paper and tinfoil and chill, covered, overnight. Seal it with a thin film of melted butter. Serve with triangles of hot toast.

Serves 4-6

CHICKEN LIVER PÂTÉ WITH WHISKY

8 oz/225 g chicken livers, chopped
3 oz/75 g butter
2 shallots, chopped
1 clove of garlic, crushed
1 teaspoon mixed herbs
1 medium gherkin, finely chopped
1 teaspoon Dijon mustard
1 tablespoon whisky
dash of Worcestershire sauce
salt and freshly ground black pepper
1 egg, lightly beaten

Sauté the shallots in the butter until they are transparent.
Add the chicken livers, stir, then add the garlic.
Cook over low heat for about 5 minutes, or until the livers
are slightly browned on the outside, but still pink within.
Add the mixed herbs, gherkin, mustard, whisky, Worcester-
shire sauce, salt and plenty of freshly ground black pepper.
Cook for another 1-3 minutes, take off the heat and add the
egg.
Put the mixture into an electric blender or mixer and blend
at high speed for 30 seconds.
Put the mixture into an ovenproof dish, cover with
greaseproof paper, a lid or tinfoil, and stand in a roasting
dish two-thirds filled with water. Bake the pâté in a
preheated oven (350°F/180°C/Gas Mark 4) for 1 hour.
Cool it under a heavy weight overnight.
Serve cold with hot triangles of toast.
Serves 4-6

PIGEON PÂTÉ

6 pigeon breasts
2 oz/50 g butter
1 large onion, chopped
4 cloves of garlic, crushed
4 oz/100 g pork, minced
4 oz/100 g ox liver, minced
4 oz/100 g streaky bacon, finely chopped
4 oz/100 g chicken livers, trimmed and chopped
1 tablespoon brandy
2 glasses of red wine
1 tablespoon double cream
salt and freshly ground black pepper

Finely dice the pigeon breasts.
Melt the butter in a deep pan, sauté the onion until transparent. Add the garlic, pigeon breasts, pork, ox liver, bacon and chicken livers.
Simmer for 1 hour over low heat, stirring frequently.
Preheat the oven to 275°F/140°C/Gas Mark 1.
Stir in the brandy, wine and cream and cook for a further 5 minutes, stirring. Season, then transfer the mixture to an ovenproof terrine or pâté dish. Cover with greaseproof paper and tinfoil and stand in a roasting dish two-thirds filled with water.
Cook for 1½-2 hours.
Remove the tinfoil and cool under a heavy weight overnight.
Serves 10-12

GAME PÂTÉ

8 oz/225 g uncooked hare or rabbit
4 oz/100 g fat bacon, diced
3 tablespoons brandy
6 oz/175 g veal, minced
6 oz/175 g pork, minced
1 egg
pinch of nutmeg
salt and freshly ground black pepper

Cut the game into small pieces and place it in a bowl with the bacon and the brandy. Marinate for 1 hour.
Coarsely blend it in an electric blender with the veal and the pork. Add the egg, nutmeg, salt and pepper and blend at maximum speed until the mixture is smooth.
Put the mixture into a lightly buttered ovenproof dish or meat loaf tin, cover it with greaseproof paper and tinfoil and stand in a roasting dish two-thirds filled with water.
Bake in a preheated oven at 400°F/200°C/Gas Mark 6 for 1 hour.
Remove the tinfoil and cool under a heavy weight overnight.
Serves 4-6

COUNTRY PÂTÉ

4 oz/100 g pigs' liver
3 oz/75 g toasted breadcrumbs
12 oz/350 g sausage meat
1 teaspoon Dijon mustard
cayenne pepper
dash of Worcestershire sauce
1 clove of garlic, crushed
1 egg yolk
salt and freshly ground black pepper

Cut the liver into narrow strips, put it into a saucepan, pour boiling water over it, then simmer for 4-5 minutes.
Drain and pat the liver dry.
Mix the breadcrumbs with the sausage meat and add the

mustard, cayenne pepper, Worcestershire sauce, garlic, salt
and plenty of freshly ground black pepper. Fold in the egg
yolk, making sure that it is thoroughly mixed.
Grease a 1 lb/450 g meat-loaf tin and pack in the pâté
mixture. Cover it with greaseproof paper and tinfoil. Stand
the tin in a roasting dish half filled with water. Cook in a
moderate oven (350°F/180°C/Gas Mark 4) for 1½ hours.
Remove the tinfoil and cool the pâté under a heavy weight
for 1 hour. Remove the weight and chill overnight.
Serve with crusty French bread or brown bread.
Serves 6-8

LIVER PÂTÉ IN ASPIC

4 oz/100 g calves' liver, minced
4 oz/100 g chicken or pigs' liver, minced
¼ pint/150 ml béchamel sauce, see page 270
pinch of mixed dried herbs
pinch of ground mace
3½ oz/100 g tender sweet bacon
1½ lb/900 ml aspic jelly or consommé
1 bay leaf
salt and freshly ground black pepper

Mix the calves' and the pigs' liver with the béchamel sauce,
add the dried herbs, the mace, salt and plenty of freshly
ground black pepper. In an electric blender or mixer blend
the mixture until it is very smooth.
Cut the bacon into small cubes and fold them into the liver
mixture. Pour the mixture into a meat-loaf tin or an
ovenproof dish and cover with greaseproof paper and tinfoil.
Stand the dish in a roasting dish half filled with water. Bake
at 350°F/180°C/Gas Mark 4 for 1 hour.
Cool under a heavy weight overnight.
The next day remove the foil and the greaseproof paper and
fill the top of the dish with cold, but still liquid, aspic jelly or
consommé. Decorate it with a bay leaf and chill until the
aspic is set.
Serve with toast or French bread.
Serves 6-8

LAMB AND SPINACH PÂTÉ

2¾ lb/1.1 kg boned shoulder of lamb
1 tablespoon shortening or lard
9 oz/250 g lean bacon
1 oz/25 g plain flour
8 fl oz/225 ml milk
1 teaspoon nutmeg, freshly ground
9 oz/250 g spinach, cooked, drained and chopped
1 egg, lightly beaten
bacon strips to line a meat-loaf or pâté dish
salt and freshly ground black pepper

for the marinade
2 medium onions, sliced
½ teaspoon dried rosemary, OR
1 teaspoon crushed fresh rosemary
4 cloves of garlic, crushed
¼ pint/150 ml olive oil
1 tablespoon wine vinegar
salt and freshly ground black pepper

Cut the shoulder of lamb into long strips, trimming off any excess fat.

In a large bowl mix together all the ingredients for the marinade and stir in the lamb, making sure all strips are well coated with the marinade. Leave it overnight in a cool place, stirring occasionally.

The following day take a large heavy saucepan, add the shortening and heat. Cut the bacon into thin slices and brown over moderate heat. Add the flour, stirring, and pour in the milk. Stir until the sauce thickens, then add the nutmeg and the lightly beaten egg.

Remove the pan from the heat and add the spinach. Mix well and add a little salt.

Grease a meat-loaf or pâté dish and line the bottom and the sides with bacon strips. Reserve 2 strips to cover the pâté when the dish is filled. Arrange the slices of lamb along the sides and across the ends, forming a hollow well in the middle. Spoon in the bacon and spinach mixture and cover it with the rest of the lamb. The whole of the mixture should be encased in the lamb. Lay the remaining strips over the top to seal.

Cook for 2 hours in a preheated medium oven (375°F/190°C/Gas Mark 5).

Cool, then remove the pâté from the dish and refrigerate. Serve cold cut into thin slices.

Serve with toast and garnish with gherkins and radishes.

Serves 8-10

HASTY PÂTÉ

1 lb/450 g German liver sausage
1 tablespoon brandy
1 clove of garlic, crushed
¼ pint/150 ml double cream
1 bay leaf
¼ teaspoon dried sage
¼ teaspoon dried thyme
¼ teaspoon dried mixed herbs
salt and freshly ground black pepper

Skin the liver sausage and mash it with a fork.

Gradually work in the brandy and the cream. Add the crushed garlic, sage, thyme, mixed herbs, salt and plenty of freshly ground black pepper.

Pack the pâté into a mould or a small dish, smooth the top with a knife blade and garnish with the bay leaf. Chill, covered, overnight.

Serve with hot toast or brown bread.

Serves 4-6

Poultry

The word 'chicken' is the generic term describing the young domestic or barnyard fowl, a descendant of the wild jungle fowl of eastern Asia. In modern idiom it includes everything from the very young chicken to the large hen only suitable for the stockpot.

The name 'turkey' was first given in England to the guinea fowl, which was originally introduced from West Africa. Turkeys, as we know them today, were brought to Europe from Mexico by the Spaniards in 1524. In the United States turkeys are eaten traditionally at Thanksgiving, as well as Christmas. England considers the turkey a 'Christmas bird', although it is available throughout the year.

Poultry is very low in cholesterol; it contains iron and vitamin B.

4 oz/100 g cooked chicken contain 144 calories.
4 oz/100 g cooked turkey contain 230 calories.

COCKTAIL POULET 'MADRAS'

14 oz/400 g chicken breasts, cooked, skins removed
2 stem ginger in syrup
1 small tin mandarin oranges
juice and grated rind of 1 orange
1 oz/25 g pistachio nuts, coarsely chopped
5 fl oz/150 ml double cream
1 tablespoon curry powder
salt
crisp lettuce leaves

Cut the chicken breasts into fine strips.
Drain the ginger, but reserve the syrup. Finely chop the ginger.
Drain the mandarins, discard the juice and, in a bowl, mix them with the chicken strips, grated orange rind and pistachio nuts.
Line 4 glasses, or salad bowls, with lettuce leaves and pile the mixture on them.
In a small bowl whisk the cream until stiff, but not too dry, slowly add the orange juice and a little of the ginger syrup.
Blend well, then add the curry powder and salt to taste. Blend again and pour the sauce over the chicken cocktail. Do not mix.
Serve cold.
Serves 4

SMOKED CHICKEN AND PEAR SALAD

12 strips of lean smoked chicken, skin removed
(available from large delicatessen stores)
2 ripe pears, quartered, peeled and cored
2 slices of white bread
juice of half a lemon
5 oz/150 g cottage cheese
2 oz/50 g walnuts, chopped
oil for frying
cayenne pepper
salt
bunch of watercress, washed, stems removed
1 tablespoon parsley, finely chopped

Remove the crusts from the bread and cut the bread into small cubes.

Toss the pears in lemon juice to prevent discolouration.

In a frying-pan heat the oil and fry the bread cubes, turning frequently, so they brown on all sides. When golden brown, remove them with a slotted spoon and drain on absorbent kitchen paper.

In a small bowl blend the cottage cheese with the walnuts and season with cayenne pepper and salt.

Spread the watercress in one layer at the bottom of a serving platter. Arrange the strips of chicken over the watercress and cover with the diced pears. Spoon the cottage cheese mixture evenly over the pears, then sprinkle the top with parsley and the fried bread *croûtons*.

Serve cold.

Serves 6

SMOKED CHICKEN AND BLUE CHEESE SALAD

1 lb/450 g smoked chicken breasts, boned, skin removed
(available from large delicatessen stores)
½ head of iceberg lettuce
bunch of watercress
1 small avocado
2 eggs, hard-boiled
3 rashers of bacon
1 tablespoon lemon juice
6 oz/175 g blue cheese, cut into 4 slices
2 tomatoes, cut into wedges
French dressing, see page 265

Chop the lettuce, remove the stems from the watercress and chop the leaves.
With a stainless steel knife peel the avocado, remove the stone and slice the flesh.
Slice the chicken breasts and chop the eggs.
Grill the bacon until golden brown, drain on absorbent kitchen paper and crumble.
In a bowl combine the lettuce and the watercress. Chill, covered for 1-3 hours.
In a small bowl gently blend the avocado and lemon juice and chill, covered, for 1-3 hours.
Transfer the green salad to a chilled serving platter and arrange on it the chicken, the cheese and the tomatoes. Pile the avocado in the centre and sprinkle with the eggs and the bacon.
Drizzle French dressing over the salad.
Serves 4-6

CHICKEN SALAD 'CHINOISE'

1 lb/450 g chicken breasts, cooked, boned and shredded
2 tablespoons peanut oil
10 oz/275 g Chinese noodles
8 oz/225 g bean sprouts
3 oz/75 g carrot, scraped and thinly sliced
4 spring onions, cut lengthwise into small strips
3 oz/75 g cucumber, peeled, seeded and thinly sliced
1 (15 oz/425 g) tin baby corn
(available at oriental shops or delicatessens)
2 tablespoons sesame oil
1 tablespoon soya sauce
¼ teaspoon powdered ginger
freshly ground black pepper

In a large saucepan bring water to boil, add 1 tablespoon of peanut oil and the noodles. Cook until they are 'al dente'.
Drain in a colander, rinse under running cold water and drain again. Transfer the noodles to a large platter.
Mix the shredded chicken breasts with the noodles.
In a saucepan of boiling water blanch the bean sprouts for 30 seconds, drain in a colander, refresh under running cold water and drain again.
Add the bean sprouts, carrot, spring onion, cucumber and baby corn to the chicken and noodle mixture and toss.
Blend 1 tablespoon of peanut oil with the sesame oil, add soya sauce, ginger, and black pepper. Whisk until well blended.
Spoon the dressing over the chicken and noodle salad. Toss again.
Serve at room temperature.
Serves 4-6

CHOPPED CHICKEN LIVERS

8 oz/225 g chicken livers, trimmed and chopped
2 oz/50 g butter
1 small onion, chopped
salt and freshly ground black pepper
1 teaspoon capers, chopped
1 egg, hard-boiled and chopped

In a heavy saucepan melt half of the butter. Sauté the onion until transparent.

With a slotted spoon transfer the onion to drain on absorbent kitchen paper.

Add the remaining butter to the butter the onion has been fried in and sauté the livers, stirring, until brown on the outside but still a little pink within. Season with salt and plenty of freshly ground black pepper.

Place the onions and the livers in an electric blender or mixer and coarsely blend for 30 seconds.

In a bowl combine the livers, capers and chopped hard-boiled egg. Mix well, correct the seasoning and chill for 1 hour.

Serve with hot buttered toast.

Serves 2-4

TURKEY AND STRAWBERRY COCKTAIL

The unusual combination of strawberries and turkey
makes this cocktail an interesting starter.

14 oz/400 g lean turkey steaks
½ teaspoon dried thyme
1 oz/25 g butter
9 oz/250 g fresh strawberries
5 fl oz/150 ml double cream
2 tablespoons mayonnaise, see page 266
1 tablespoon lemon juice
1 teaspoon Dijon mustard
1 tablespoon tomato ketchup
dash of Worcestershire sauce
1 tablespoon brandy
salt and freshly ground white pepper
leaves of 1 small round lettuce

Flatten the turkey steaks with a wooden mallet between two sheets of greaseproof paper. Rub them with the thyme, freshly ground white pepper and salt.

In a heavy saucepan heat the butter and fry the steaks for 2 minutes on each side, or until cooked. Remove them with a slotted spoon and drain on absorbent kitchen paper. Set aside to cool, then cut them into thin strips.

Wash and drain the strawberries, removing the stalks, and cut them in half.

Wash and dry the lettuce and line 4 individual dishes or salad plates with the leaves.

Mix the turkey with the strawberries and divide it into 4 individual portions.

In a small bowl whisk the cream until firm, but not too dry; slowly add the mayonnaise, mustard, lemon juice, tomato ketchup, Worcestershire sauce and brandy. Whisk until all the ingredients are thoroughly combined.

Add freshly ground white pepper and salt to taste and pour the sauce over the turkey and strawberry portions. Do not mix.

Serve cold.

Serves 4

TIPSY TURKEY SALAD

9 oz/250 g turkey breasts
1 oz/25 g butter
2 tablespoons dry white wine
2 grapefruit
2 teaspoons gin
1 tablespoon green peppercorns
3 tablespoons walnut or nut oil
2 tablespoons white wine vinegar
2 small radicchio salads
2 tablespoons orange juice
5 fl oz/142 ml sour cream
1 tablespoon brandy
salt and freshly ground white pepper

Flatten the turkey breasts with a wooden mallet between two sheets of greaseproof paper. Rub salt and plenty of freshly ground white pepper into the breasts.

Heat the butter in a heavy pan and gently fry the breasts until they are golden on both sides. Add the wine and sauté the breasts for a further 25 minutes with the lid on.

With a slotted spoon remove the breasts, cool and cut into ½ inch/1 cm strips.

Peel the grapefruit, removing all membrane and cut into small segments. Place the segments into a bowl, pour the gin over them, soak for 20 minutes, then drain.

In a separate bowl blend the oil with the vinegar.

Mix the turkey breasts with the grapefruit segments and sprinkle with green peppercorns.

Wash and dry the radicchios and line 4 individual bowls or salad plates with the leaves. Mound the turkey and grapefruit mixture in the centre of the bowls or plates and spoon the oil and vinegar dressing over.

Blend the orange juice with the sour cream, whisk in the brandy and serve the sauce separately.

Serve cold.

Serves 4

Quiche

The quiche, also known as 'kiche', was originally made of bread dough but over the years this gradually changed to pastry. It has been claimed that it first came from Germany, since in Germany the quiche is also known as 'Kuchen' from which the word 'kiche' could have come.

There is an enormous variety of fillings for the pastry shell but it is the quiche from Lorraine that has become most widely known.

Like all pastries, the quiche is high in calories.

QUICHE PASTRY

7½ oz/212 g frozen shortcrust pastry, OR
8 oz/225 g flour
4 oz/100 g butter
pinch of salt
1-2 tablespoons iced water

Sift the flour into a mixing bowl and with your fingertips rub
in the butter until the mixture resembles fine breadcrumbs.
Add a pinch of salt, then enough iced water to achieve the
consistency of a firm paste.
Chill for about 1 hour.
Preheat the oven to 375°F/190°C/Gas Mark 5.
Roll out the pastry as thinly as possible and line a tin.
Prick the bottom with a fork.
Fill the pastry case with the quiche filling.
Serves 4

SPINACH QUICHE

Prepared pastry case
½ pint/300 ml single cream
6 oz/175 g Cheddar cheese, grated
2 tablespoons cooked spinach, finely chopped
1 teaspoon powdered mustard
3 large eggs, beaten
salt and freshly ground black pepper

In a bowl mix the cream, grated cheese and spinach.
Stir the beaten eggs into the mixture. Add the salt, pepper
and mustard and blend well.
Pour the mixture into the quiche case and place it on a hot
baking sheet in the preheated oven.
Bake for 35-40 minutes. Lift out gently and let it cool.
Serve at room temperature.
Serves 4

ONION AND ANCHOVY QUICHE

Prepared pastry case, see page 235
2 lb/1 kg onions, finely chopped
4 fl oz/100 ml olive oil
small tin of anchovies, drained
salt and freshly ground black pepper

In a heavy saucepan cook the onions in 3 tablespoons of the olive oil until they are quite soft but not brown.
Spoon the onions into the pastry case.
Rinse the anchovy fillets in water to remove excess salt and make a lattice pattern over the onions. Sprinkle the surface with a little salt and freshly ground pepper.
Drizzle the remaining oil over the top and bake in a hot oven (425°F/220°C/Gas Mark 7) for 15-20 minutes.
Serve hot.
Serves 4

QUICHE LORRAINE

Prepared pastry case, see page 235
½ oz/15 g butter
6 rashers streaky bacon, chopped
2 eggs, beaten
½ pint/275 ml single cream
salt and freshly ground black pepper
a little butter

Heat the butter in a small pan, add the chopped bacon and fry until golden. Sprinkle it over the pastry.
Mix the beaten eggs with the cream, add salt and pepper, blend again and pour this mixture over the bacon in the prepared pastry case.
Add little dots of butter and bake it in the oven for 30 minutes, or until the top is browned.
Serves 4

Snails

The snail, a great favourite of some, is detested by others.

The size of the snail was of great importance to the ancient Romans, who established snail farms where the molluscs were fed on milk and wine until they were too fat to retreat to their shells.

Recipes of the sixteenth and seventeenth centuries refer to 'snail pie' as being particularly beneficial to health; snail water, a rather repulsive liquid distilled from the snail when boiled with earthworm and wine, was thought to cure certain illnesses.

Today the best snails are considered those which are grown in French vineyards, particularly in Burgundy, and fed on vine leaves.

In some parts of France, Italy and Spain snails are still sold alive in the markets. But preparing them is a time-consuming and bothersome procedure; they have to be kept in an earthenware pot for a week; they have to be washed several times until they froth: the veils, which close the opening have to be removed with a sharp knife. And finally, they have to be cooked for hours.

It is not surprising that today even the most dedicated French cooks buy their snails prepared and ready for cooking. Tinned snails are available in most delicatessen shops and large supermarkets and are easy to prepare.

4 oz/100 g snail flesh contain 83 calories.

SNAILS IN HERB BUTTER

4 dozen snails, cleaned and prepared, with their shells
3½ oz/100 g butter
4 cloves of garlic
3 tablespoons parsley, finely chopped
2 tablespoons soft breadcrumbs
freshly ground black pepper

Put the cleaned and prepared snails back into their shells.
Pound together the butter, garlic, parsley and breadcrumbs.
Pound into a smooth paste and season with plenty of freshly
ground black pepper. Put a little of this mixture into each
shell.
Place a dozen snails on 4 individual ovenproof plates and put
them in a hot oven (475°F/240°C/Gas Mark 9).
Heat until the butter is sizzling.
Serve hot in their shells.
Serves 4

SNAILS IN RED WINE

4 dozen snails, cleaned and prepared, shells discarded
1½ pints/900 ml red wine
3 cloves of garlic, crushed
½ red pepper, seeded and chopped
2 onions, chopped
2 cloves
1 bay leaf
pinch of marjoram
salt and freshly ground black pepper

In a large saucepan bring the wine, garlic and onion to boil.
As soon as the mixture reaches boiling point, add the red
pepper, cloves, bay leaf, marjoram and snails.
Cook over moderate heat for 25-30 minutes.
Season with salt and pepper and serve it, altogether, in a
soup tureen.
Serves 4

SNAILS IN MUSHROOMS

1 dozen snails, prepared, shells discarded
1 dozen mushrooms with caps about
1½ inch/4 cm in diameter
2 oz/50 g butter, softened
2 tablespoons dry sherry
1 oz/25 g Parmesan cheese, grated
1 tablespoon fresh tarragon, chopped, OR
1 teaspoon dried tarragon
1 tablespoon fresh sage, chopped, OR
1 teaspoon dried sage
1 clove of garlic, crushed
1 teaspoon fresh chives, chopped
1 oz/25 g sliced almonds
salt and freshly ground black pepper

Rinse the snails and pat them dry.

Remove the stems from the mushrooms and discard.

In a bowl combine the butter, sherry, Parmesan, tarragon, sage, garlic, chives, salt and pepper. Blend this mixture well and divide it between the mushroom caps.

Put one snail on each mushroom, topping the snails with any remaining mixture.

Sprinkle the mushrooms with the Parmesan and the almonds.

Arrange the mushrooms in one layer on a flat pan and grill them under a hot grill about 5 inches/15 cm away from the heat for 3 minutes, or until they begin to bubble.

Serve hot.

Serves 4

Spinach

Spinach is thought to have originated in Persia. Unknown to the Romans, it was brought to Europe by the Moors, and was introduced to European cookery by the Dutch.

A late fourteenth century recipe has it 'parboiled in water, drained, fried in clean oil, with no more than a little spice powder on it'. While to the Elizabethans a salad of boiled spinach was regarded as a great favourite.

In the 1920s the popularity of spinach went into decline, probably because of its association with the nursery and the well-propounded theory that its high iron content was particularly beneficial for children. But today spinach is a vegetable enjoyed by many throughout the year.

It contains a fair amount of vitamins A, C and K, iron and potassium.

4 oz/100 g spinach contains 23 calories.

SPINACH SALAD WITH BACON AND YOGHURT

Spinach salad is very popular in America. The following recipes, given to me by American friends, are easy to prepare. But always make sure to use only very young spinach leaves.

1 lb/450 g fresh young spinach leaves, stalks removed
4 rashers bacon, rinds removed

for the dressing
2 tablespoons plain yoghurt
2 tablespoons double cream
2 tablespoons olive oil
½ tablespoon lemon juice
1½ teaspoons Dijon mustard
1 clove of garlic, crushed
½ teaspoon sugar
salt and freshly ground black pepper

Grill or fry the bacon until it is very crisp. Cool on absorbent kitchen paper, then chop or crumble it into small bits.
Wash the spinach leaves and pat them dry.
In a bowl mix the yoghurt, double cream, oil, lemon juice, mustard, garlic, sugar, salt and pepper.
Whisk all the ingredients until they are thoroughly blended.
Pour the dressing over the spinach and transfer it to a large wooden bowl.
Toss the salad several times until all the leaves are coated in the dressing and sprinkle it with bacon bits.
Serves 4

SPINACH AND STILTON SALAD

1 lb/450 g young spinach leaves, stalks removed
2 oz/50 g Stilton, or Roquefort cheese, crumbled
1 tablespoon sesame seeds

for the dressing
1 teaspoon Dijon mustard
2 teaspoons tarragon vinegar
4 tablespoons sunflower oil
pinch of sugar
dash of tabasco sauce
salt and freshly ground black pepper

Wash the spinach leaves and pat dry. Tear them into small bits.
Toast the sesame seeds in a moderate oven (325°F/160°C/ Gas mark 3) for about 20 minutes.
Place the salad into a large wooden salad bowl. Sprinkle the seeds over the spinach.
In a separate bowl combine the mustard, vinegar, salt, sugar, tabasco sauce and pepper. Whisk, then add the oil in a slow stream, whisking until the mixture emulsifies.
Pour the dressing over the spinach and toss well until all the leaves are coated.
Serves 4

SPINACH AND CARROT SALAD

1 lb/450 g fresh young spinach leaves, stalks removed
1 lb/450 g young carrots, grated
2 hard-boiled eggs, chopped
juice of 1 lemon
¼ pint/150 ml mayonnaise, see page 266
paprika
salt and freshly ground black pepper

Wash the spinach leaves and pat dry. Tear them into small pieces. In a large bowl mix the spinach with the carrots.
In a separate bowl blend the lemon juice with the mayonnaise, season and spoon the dressing over the spinach and carrot mixture.
Toss until all the leaves are coated with the dressing.
Sprinkle over with chopped eggs and dust with paprika.
Serves 4

SPINACH AND TOMATO SALAD

1 lb/450 g fresh young spinach leaves, stalks removed
3-4 tomatoes, peeled, seeded and chopped
2 hard-boiled eggs, chopped
oregano
pinch of sugar
1 teaspoon Dijon mustard
4 fl oz/100 ml single cream
juice of 1 lemon
salt and freshly ground black pepper

Wash the spinach leaves and pat dry. Tear them into small pieces.
In a large bowl combine the spinach and chopped tomatoes.
In a separate bowl blend the oregano, sugar, mustard, cream, lemon, salt and pepper. Blend until the mixture is smooth, then spoon it over the spinach salad and toss until all the leaves are coated with the dressing.
Sprinkle over with chopped eggs.
Serves 4

SPINACH PIE

1 pastry case, 8 inches/20 cm
12 oz/350 g frozen spinach
salt and freshly ground black pepper
1 oz/25 g butter
8 oz/225 g cottage cheese
2 oz/50 g Parmesan cheese, grated
6 tablespoons double cream
3 eggs, lightly beaten
grated nutmeg
dash of Worcestershire sauce

Line a pie dish or tin with the pastry, fluting the edges.
Chill for about 1 hour.
Prick the bottom with a fork and bake 'blind' in a hot oven at 450°F/230°C/Gas Mark 8 for 15 minutes, or until just long enough to set the crust without browning it. Set aside to cool.
Cook the spinach with salt and pepper, add the butter and stir. Drain thoroughly.
In a bowl blend the spinach with the cottage cheese, Parmesan, cream, beaten eggs, nutmeg, Worcestershire sauce and a little more salt and pepper.
Spread the mixture in the pastry shell and bake in a moderate oven at 375°F/190°C/Gas Mark 5 for 25-30 minutes, or until the crust is brown and the cheese mixture has set.
Serve hot or cold.
Serves 4-6

CHILLED SPINACH SOUP

1 lb/450 g fresh spinach, or 14 oz/400 g frozen spinach
spinach water
½ pint/300 ml chicken stock
1½ tablespoons lemon juice
salt and freshly ground white pepper
1 (5 fl oz/142 ml) carton sour cream
¼ teaspoon onion, finely grated
¼ cucumber, peeled, seeded and diced

Cook the spinach in a little water until tender. Cook the frozen spinach according to instructions.

Drain, reserving the spinach water.

Put the spinach into an electric blender or mixer and blend until smooth. Return the spinach to the saucepan. Add the spinach water and the stock and bring to boil, then remove from the heat.

Add the lemon juice, salt and pepper.

Stir and leave to cool, then place, covered, in the refrigerator for several hours.

An hour before serving mix in the sour cream, onion and cucumber. Blend well and correct the seasoning.

Serve chilled in chilled bowls or soup plates.

Serves 4

Tomato

By the time the Spaniards conquered South America, cultivation had already improved the original weed that was the tomato. The type of tomato that was introduced to Europe in the middle of the sixteenth century by the Spaniards appeared to have been yellow, hence the name 'Golden Apple' by which the tomato was first known. Because of their supposed aphrodisiac properties, tomatoes became known as 'Apples of Love'. While the Spaniards ate the tomato with oil and vinegar, in sixteenth-century England the tomato was viewed with great suspicion. It was known to be of the family of nightshade and thought to be a highly dangerous food. Tomatoes were cultivated in gardens only as a decorative curiosity, and it was not until the nineteenth century that tomatoes were cautiously admitted into English kitchens.

The early settlers reintroduced the cultivated tomato to America, but it didn't gain wide popularity until the middle of the nineteenth century.

Today the tomato is grown throughout the world and the number of varieties is vast.

Tomatoes are high in vitamins A, K, C and potassium.

4 oz/100 g tomato contains 19 calories.

Tips
■ Peel the tomatoes after immersing them for 10-30 seconds in boiling water.

TOMATOES À LA GRÈCQUE

8 medium tomatoes
1 large onion, finely chopped
1 tablespoon fresh chives, chopped, OR
1 tablespoon green spring onion tops, finely chopped
1 teaspoon fresh chervil, chopped, OR
½ teaspoon dried chervil
1 teaspoon fresh basil, chopped, OR
½ teaspoon dried basil
pinch of dried tarragon
1 clove of garlic, crushed
½ pint/300 ml French dressing, see page 265
1 tablespoon sultanas
finely chopped parsley
crisp lettuce leaves

Make 3 incisions from the top of the tomatoes, but do not cut through the base. With a small spoon scoop out the core and the seeds. Put the tomatoes upside-down in a dish or on a plate and let them drain in the refrigerator.

In a bowl mix the onion, all the herbs, the garlic and the French dressing. Leave for several hours, covered, in a cool place.

Plunge the sultanas into boiling water and soak for 5 minutes. Drain and add to the onion and dressing.

Strain the dressing through a sieve and remove the garlic.

Fill the tomatoes with the stuffing and sprinkle chopped parsley across the top of each incision.

Just before serving pour a little dressing over each tomato.

Serve cold on a bed of crisp lettuce leaves.

Serves 4

BEL'S QUICK TOMATO STARTER

This recipe was given to me by a friend who is able to invent and produce the most appetizing dishes at a moment's notice.

4 large tomatoes
4 eggs, hard-boiled
4 tablespoons parsley, finely chopped
4 tablespoons French dressing, see page 265
4 crisp lettuce leaves

Cut the eggs into slices with an egg cutter.
Place the tomatoes on a chopping board, stem side down, and cut them into slices from the top without cutting through the base.
Put an egg slice in between each of the tomato slices.
Chop up the remaining egg slices and set aside.
Stand the egg-stuffed tomato on a chilled salad plate lined with a crisp lettuce leaf, pour 1 tablespoon French dressing and sprinkle 1 tablespoon parsley over each tomato.
Garnish with any remaining chopped egg.
Serve very cold.
Serves 4

TOMATO ROSES

12 small, or 6 large tomatoes, peeled
8 oz/225 g prawns, cooked and peeled
5 fl oz/142 ml sour cream
1 tablespoon fresh dill, chopped, OR
1¼ teaspoons dried dill weed
cayenne pepper
1 teaspoon Dijon mustard
1 teaspoon lemon juice
¼ teaspoon sugar
salt and freshly ground white pepper
crisp lettuce leaves

Place the tomatoes on a wooden board, stalk side down, and quarter them carefully without cutting through the base.
Gently spread the petals apart and with a rounded teaspoon

scoop out the core and seeds. Fold them together and stand the tomatoes upside-down to drain.

In a bowl mix the sour cream with the dill, cayenne, mustard, lemon juice, sugar, salt and white pepper. Fold in the prawns and mix well.

Line 6 chilled individual salad plates with lettuce leaves.

Gently spread out the 4 petals of the tomatoes. Fill the inside of each tomato with the prawn mixture. Dust with a little cayenne.

Serve cold.

Serves 6

ACCORDION TOMATOES

6 large firm tomatoes, peeled
1 small tin salmon, drained
3 hard-boiled eggs
2 teaspoons parsley, chopped
½ teaspoon fresh tarragon, chopped, OR
pinch of dried tarragon
¼ pint/150 ml mayonnaise, see page 266
crisp lettuce leaves
2 carrots, grated
few sprigs of watercress

Place the tomatoes on a wooden board, stalk side down, and cut them into thin slices from the top without cutting through the base.

Flake the salmon with a fork; chop the eggs finely. In a bowl combine the salmon, eggs, parsley, tarragon and the mayonnaise. Blend until the mixture is smooth.

Line 6 chilled individual salad plates with the lettuce leaves and place a tomato on each. With a small spoon push some of the salmon mayonnaise between the slices of the tomatoes.

Decorate each plate with grated carrot and sprigs of watercress.

Serve cold.

Serves 6

TOMATOES CASTELNAU

4 large, or 8 small tomatoes, peeled
4 hearts of palm

for the sauce
5 fl oz/142 ml single cream
½ teaspoon fresh chives, chopped
1 teaspoon fresh parsley, chopped
1 teaspoon fresh basil, chopped
1 teaspoon Dijon mustard
1 teaspoon lemon juice
1 spring onion, finely chopped
1 teaspoon fresh dill, chopped, OR
½ teaspoon dried dill weed
pinch of sugar
dash of cayenne pepper
salt and freshly ground white pepper

Slice the peeled tomatoes and arrange them on 4 chilled individual salad plates.

Cut the hearts of palm into ½ inch/1 cm rounds, and arrange them with the tomatoes.

In a bowl mix the cream with the mustard, lemon juice, spring onion and all the herbs. Add the sugar, cayenne, salt and white pepper and blend well.

Just before serving spoon the sauce over the tomatoes and the hearts of palm.

Serve chilled.

Serves 4

TOMATO AND HEARTS OF PALM SALAD

8 oz/225 g fresh young spinach, stalks removed
2 tablespoons fresh basil leaves, chopped
¼ pint/150 ml French dressing, see page 265
4 tomatoes, peeled
1 (14 oz/400 g) tin hearts of palm
5 oz/150 g black olives, pitted
1 round lettuce, washed, dried and separated into leaves

Blend the chopped basil leaves into the French dressing. Set aside.

Wash the spinach and pat it dry. Core and cut the tomatoes into wedges. Drain the hearts of palm and cut them into 1 inch/2.5 cm pieces.

Line a large serving dish with the spinach and lettuce leaves. Arrange the tomatoes and hearts of palm in the centre over the green salad. Sprinkle with the olives.

Serve the French dressing separately.

Serves 4

TOMATO SALAD WITH CHICK-PEA DRESSING

1 (15½ oz/440 g) tin chick-peas, drained
4 large tomatoes, peeled
4 tablespoons lemon juice
4 tablespoons cold water
2 cloves of garlic, crushed
¾ teaspoon salt (or less, according to taste)
¼ pint/150 ml vegetable oil
1 tablespoon parsley, finely chopped
paprika

In an electric blender or mixer blend the chick-peas with the lemon juice, water, garlic and salt until the mixture is smooth. With the motor running, add the oil in a steady stream. Continue to blend until the mixture is thoroughly combined.

Transfer the mixture to a bowl and let it stand, covered, in a cool place for 1 hour.

Core and cut the tomatoes into ½ inch/1 cm slices.

Spoon half of the chick-pea dressing on each of 4 individual plates. Press the tomato slices slightly into the dressing.

Pour the rest of the dressing over the tomatoes and garnish each serving with parsley and a dusting of paprika.

Serve at room temperature.

Serves 4

TOMATO SORBET WITH RED PEPPER

1 lb/450 g ripe tomatoes, peeled
1 red pepper
1 sprig fresh mint, coarsely chopped
2 sprigs dill, coarsely chopped, OR
½ teaspoon dried dill
white of 1 egg
dash of tabasco sauce
6 fl oz/150 ml dry white wine
salt and freshly ground white pepper
fresh chives or fresh parsley, chopped

Core and halve the red pepper and place it under a hot grill until the skin begins to blister. Leave to cool; remove the skin and chop the pepper.
Quarter the tomatoes, remove cores and seeds. Place the tomatoes, red pepper, dill and mint in an electric blender or mixer. Blend, then add the wine, egg white, tabasco, white pepper and salt to taste.
Pour the mixture into a flat dish and place it into the deep-freezing part of the refrigerator for at least 3 hours.
Stir from time to time with a fork to prevent the formation of ice crystals.
Serve chilled in chilled glasses or small bowls. Garnish with a sprinkling of chopped chives or parsley.
Serves 4

TOMATOES STUFFED WITH GUACAMOLE

6 large ripe tomatoes
2 ripe avocados
2 tablespoons lemon juice
¾ teaspoon chilli powder
1 small onion, finely chopped
1 tablespoon celery, finely chopped
salt and freshly ground black pepper

Cut off the tops of the tomatoes to make lids and scoop out the seeds and cores with a rounded teaspoon. Turn the tomatoes upside-down to drain. Strain the seeds and reserve the juice. With a stainless steel knife halve the avocados, and peel and stone them.

In a bowl mix the avocado halves, the reserved tomato juice, lemon juice, chilli powder, onion, celery, salt and pepper. With a silver fork or a wooden spatula mash it into a smooth purée.

Taste for seasoning, cover tightly and chill until ready for serving.

Fill the tomatoes with the avocado mixture and set the lids on top at a slant.

Serve chilled.

Serves 6

TOMATOES GERVAIS

6 large firm tomatoes, peeled
4 oz/100 g Gervais cream cheese,
or any other cream cheese
fresh chives, chopped, OR
green spring onion tops, chopped
3 tablespoons double cream
dash of cayenne pepper
salt and freshly ground white pepper

Cut off the tops of the tomatoes to make lids and scoop out the seeds and cores with a rounded teaspoon.

Discard the pulp. Turn the tomatoes upside-down to drain.

Sieve the cheese by pushing it with a wooden spoon through a sieve resting over a bowl. Add the cream, season with cayenne, salt and pepper. Blend well and add the chives or the green spring onion tops.

Sprinkle a little salt into the hollows of the tomatoes.

Fill the tomatoes with the cream cheese mixture and set the lids on top at a slant.

Sprinkle with the remaining chives and chill.

Serves 6

TOMATOES WITH FRUIT

3-4 tablespoons single cream
1 tablespoon vegetable oil
juice of 1 lemon
pinch of sugar
salt and freshly ground white pepper
pinch of cayenne pepper
pinch of celery salt
2 oranges
2 dessert apples
5 oz/150 g dark grapes
4 large firm tomatoes, peeled

In a small bowl blend the cream with the oil, lemon juice, sugar, salt and pepper, cayenne and celery salt. Whisk and set aside.
Peel the oranges and cut into small sections.
Peel, core and dice the apples.
Halve the grapes, removing all pips.
Mix the fruit.
Place the tomatoes on a wooden board, stalk side down, and make 8 cuts through the flesh from the top without cutting through the base. Press back the petals and with a rounded teaspoon scoop out the cores and seeds.
Put a large spoonful of the mixed fruit in each tomato and cover with the dressing.
Serves 4

BAKED TOMATO STUFFED WITH CUCUMBER

4-6 large firm tomatoes
1 oz/25 g butter
1 medium cucumber, peeled, seeded and diced
½ pint/300 ml béchamel sauce, see page 270
salt and freshly ground white pepper
pinch of sugar
toasted breadcrumbs

Cut off the tops of the tomatoes, scoop out the cores and
the seeds. Turn the tomatoes upside-down to drain.
In a saucepan melt the butter and add the cucumber. Stir
and cook over low heat until the cucumber softens.
Add the béchamel sauce and cook for a further 2-3 minutes
over low heat. Season with salt and pepper.
Dust the inside of the tomatoes with sugar and a little salt
and pepper. Fill the tomatoes with the cucumber mixture.
Sprinkle with breadcrumbs.
Bake in a moderate oven (350°F/180°C/Gas Mark 4) until
the tomatoes are tender.
Serve immediately.
Serves 4-6

TOMATO JELLY WITH CELERY REMOULADE

8 oz/225 g ripe tomatoes
½ onion, chopped
½ carrot, sliced
1 stalk celery, sliced
1 bay leaf
6 black peppercorns
½ teaspoon sugar
salt to taste
¾ pint/450 ml chicken stock
1 tablespoon tomato purée
juice of half a lemon
few drops of tabasco sauce
1½ (0.6 oz/16 g) packets powdered gelatine

for the celery remoulade
1 egg yolk, hard-boiled
1 egg yolk, raw
salt
½ teaspoon Dijon mustard
¼ pint/150 ml vegetable oil
1 tablespoon white wine vinegar
1 tablespoon lemon juice
2 tablespoons natural yoghurt
1 head of celery, finely sliced

Make the jelly a few hours in advance:
Chop the tomatoes and put into a saucepan with the onion, carrot, celery, bay leaf, peppercorns, sugar and salt. Mix well and increase the heat.
Add the stock and the tomato purée and bring to boil, then reduce the heat and simmer for 30 minutes.
Strain and measure. Make up to 1½ pints/900 ml with the stock.
Add the lemon juice and tabasco.
Soak the gelatine in a cup with 4 tablespoons of cold water, then stand the cup in a pan of very hot water until the gelatine has melted. Stir it into the tomato liquid, mix well, then strain again.
Pour the mixture into a rinsed ring mould and leave to cool, then chill until set.

To make the celery remoulade:
Mash the hard-boiled egg yolk in a bowl with a fork. Add the
raw yolk and mix into a paste with a wooden spoon.
Add salt and mustard.
Slowly add the oil, drop by drop, as if making a mayonnaise.
Add the vinegar and lemon juice and stir well. Mix in the
yoghurt. Blend, and stir in the finely sliced celery.

To turn out the mould, dip it briefly into hot water, then run
a thin knife blade around the edge of the mould. Invert a
plate over the top and turn the mould and the plate over
together. Give it a sharp shake to dislodge the jelly.
Fill the middle of the ring mould with the celery remoulade.
Serve chilled.
Serves 6

TOMATOES EN GELÉE

4 large, or 8 small tomatoes, peeled
¼ teaspoon onion salt
¼ teaspoon celery salt
salt and freshly ground black pepper
2 tablespoons parsley, finely chopped
1 tin consommé
1 tablespoon dry sherry
4 teaspoons sour cream
1 teaspoon onion, finely grated

Halve, core and seed the tomatoes. Chop them quite finely
and divide among 4 small individual dishes.
Dust each portion with onion and celery salt, black pepper
and salt.
Sprinkle with parsley.
Mix the consommé with the sherry and spoon the liquid over
the chopped tomatoes. Chill until set.
Top each serving with sour cream and sprinkle with grated
onion.
Serve chilled.
Serves 4

CREAMY TOMATO AND GREEN BEAN SALAD

4 tomatoes, peeled
1½ lb/675 g French green beans
¼ pint/150 ml double cream
4 tablespoons red wine vinegar
¼ teaspoon sugar
salt and freshly ground black pepper
fresh chervil, chopped
fresh parsley, chopped

Chop the tomatoes, removing seeds and cores.
Boil the beans in salted water for about 7 minutes, or until cooked but still crisp. Drain, refresh under running cold water and pat dry.
In a salad bowl lightly beat the cream: slowly add the vinegar, whisking.
Add the sugar, pepper and salt.
Whisk and fold in the beans and the tomatoes.
Garnish with chervil and parsley.
Serve very cold.
Serves 4

TOMATO MOULD WITH COTTAGE CHEESE FILLING

Fresh dill and fresh basil make the world of difference to this delicate, refreshing starter. Dried can be used if that is all that is available.

1¾ pint/750 ml tomato juice
1½ teaspoons Worcestershire sauce
6 black peppercorns
1 bay leaf
½ teaspoon salt
few drops of tabasco sauce
pinch of celery salt
1 teaspoon lemon juice
pinch of sugar
1½ tablespoons powdered gelatine
8 oz/225 g cottage cheese
1 tablespoon radishes, chopped

1 tablespoon spring onions, chopped
1 tablespoon fresh dill, chopped, OR
1 teaspoon dried dill weed
1 teaspoon fresh basil, chopped, OR
¼ teaspoon dried basil

In a heavy saucepan combine the tomato juice, Worcestershire sauce, peppercorns, bay leaf, salt, celery salt, tabasco, lemon juice and sugar. Bring the mixture to boil, then simmer, covered, for 30 minutes. Strain through a colander.

Soften the gelatine in about 2 tablespoons of water for 10 minutes, then whisk it into the hot tomato mixture until it is completely dissolved.

In a separate bowl combine the cottage cheese, radishes, spring onion, dill and basil. Mix well.

Rinse a mould and half fill it with the tomato mixture. Leave it to cool. When nearly set, spread the cottage cheese mixture over it. Pour the remaining tomato mixture over the cottage cheese. Cover loosely and chill overnight.

To turn out, dip the mould briefly into hot water, then run a thin knife blade around the edge of the mould. Invert a plate over the top and turn the plate and the mould over together. Give it a sharp shake to dislodge the mousse.

If it is a ring mould, fill the centre with watercress and chopped lettuce leaves and sprinkle with French dressing.

RATATOUILLE

2 aubergines, cut into 1 inch/2.5 cm cubes
6-8 tablespoons olive oil
2 large onions, sliced
2 peppers, seeded and sliced
2 cloves of garlic, crushed
4 courgettes, thickly sliced
4 large ripe tomatoes, peeled
salt and freshly ground black pepper
1 tablespoon parsley, finely chopped

Sprinkle the aubergines with salt and leave to drain in a colander for 30 minutes.
Heat the oil in a heavy saucepan: add the onions and cook gently until they soften. Add the peppers, aubergine, garlic and courgettes. Cover the pan and simmer for 10 minutes.
Add the tomatoes and season with plenty of freshly ground black pepper and salt.
Without replacing the lid cook over medium heat for another 15 minutes, or until the vegetables are well cooked but not mushy.
Pour the ratatouille into a serving dish and leave to cool.
Sprinkle with parsley. Serve cold.
Serves 6

HERBED TOMATO TOASTS

2¼ lb/1 kg plum tomatoes, peeled
2 cloves of garlic, crushed
1½ teaspoons fresh oregano, chopped, OR
½ teaspoon dried oregano
2 tablespoons olive oil
4 teaspoons fresh basil leaves, chopped
12 small slices wholewheat bread, toasted
salt and freshly ground black pepper

Chop the tomatoes and drain in a colander for 30 minutes. Transfer to a bowl.

In a small pan cook the garlic with the oregano in the oil over moderate heat for 30 minutes. Let the mixture cool.

Stir in the fresh basil, salt and pepper and toss lightly with the tomatoes.

Spread the mixture on slices of toast.

Serve immediately.

Serves 6

CHILLED TOMATO BOUILLON

1 oz/25 g butter
1 onion, finely chopped
2½ pints/1.5 litres tomato juice
1 bay leaf
½ stalk celery, chopped with leaves
½ teaspoon dried oregano
½ teaspoon celery salt
salt and freshly ground black pepper
6 tablespoons sour cream
fresh chives or green tops of spring onions, chopped

In a heavy saucepan melt the butter. Sauté the onion until transparent.

Add the tomato juice, bay leaf, celery, oregano, celery salt, salt and plenty of freshly ground black pepper.

Simmer, covered, over low heat for 15 minutes.

Strain the liquid through a sieve and correct the seasoning.

Cool, then place in the refrigerator overnight.

Serve chilled, in chilled soup bowls with a spoonful of sour cream floating in the centre.

Sprinkle with finely chopped chives or green spring onion tops.

Serves 6

ICED TOMATO SOUP WITH BLACK OLIVES

2 lb/900 g ripe tomatoes, peeled
2 cloves of garlic, crushed
small glass of red wine
salt to taste
freshly ground black pepper
pinch of sugar
1 tablespoon sweet paprika
2 tablespoons olive oil
2 onions, finely grated
1 small cucumber, peeled, seeded and finely chopped
12 black olives, pitted and chopped
fresh parsley, finely chopped

Finely chop the tomatoes, discarding cores and seeds.
Combine the tomatoes, garlic, wine, salt, pepper, sugar and paprika in a bowl.
Gradually mix in the oil, beating it into the mixture with a wire whisk.
Add the onions, cucumber and olives and blend well.
Chill, covered, for several hours or overnight.
Serve chilled in chilled soup bowls. Sprinkle with parsley.
Serves 4-6

Salad Dressings and Sauces

In England the earliest salad recipe was recorded about 1393:
Salad. Take parsley, sage, garlic, chibols, onions, leek, borage, mints, porray, fennel and garden cresses, rue, rosemary, purslain; lave and wash them clean; pick them, pluck them small with thine hand, and mingle them well with raw oil. Lay on vinegar and salt and serve it forth.

Vinegar was a most popular condiment in England during the Elizabethan times, and for a further hundred years vinegar was used on its own, without the complementing oil or salt. Yet, until recently, the art of salad making has never been perfected by the English.

The salad is the glory of every French dinner and the disgrace of most in England.
1846, quoted in *The Shorter Oxford English Dictionary*

If salads were an enigma to the English, so too were sauces.
France has three religions and three hundred sauces, while England has three sauces and three hundred religions, mocks an early gibe.

Sauces always have been a vital part of French cookery and all good cooks would agree with Alexandre Dumas, who said that no cook is a good cook until he has mastered the art of sauce making.

Tips

■ Mayonnaise can be kept in a tightly covered jar in the refrigerator for up to one week. Before serving, leave it to stand at room temperature for 1 hour.

■ French dressing can be kept in a tightly covered screw-top jar in the refrigerator for one week. Before serving, shake the jar vigorously.

FRENCH DRESSING
Sauce vinaigrette

salt and freshly ground black pepper
1 tablespoon white wine vinegar
3 tablespoons oil

Put the salt into a salad bowl, add freshly ground black pepper and stir in the vinegar with a wooden spoon.
Stir until the salt has dissolved. Salt will not dissolve in oil.
Add the oil in a slow stream, beating the mixture until it is emulsified.

FRENCH DRESSING WITH MUSTARD
Vinaigrette à la moutarde

salt and freshly ground black pepper
1 tablespoon white wine vinegar
1 teaspoon Dijon mustard
3 tablespoons oil

Put the salt into a salad bowl, add freshly ground black pepper and stir in the vinegar with a wooden spoon. Stir until the salt has dissolved.
Add the mustard. Add the oil in a slow stream and beat until it emulsifies.

CREAMED FRENCH DRESSING
Vinaigrette à la crème

salt and freshly ground black pepper
1 tablespoon white wine vinegar
1 teaspoon Dijon mustard (optional)
pinch of sugar
3 tablespoons double cream, lightly beaten

Put the salt into a salad bowl, add freshly ground black pepper and stir in the vinegar with a wooden spoon. Add the mustard and the sugar. Blend well and stir in the cream.

GARLIC FRENCH DRESSING

1 clove of garlic
salt
freshly ground black pepper
2 tablespoons white wine vinegar
1 tablespoon fresh lemon juice
6-8 tablespoons olive oil

In a bowl mash the garlic clove with the salt and pepper to a paste. Beat in the vinegar and the lemon juice and add the oil in a slow stream, beating the dressing until it is well combined.

MAYONNAISE

See illustration

2 large egg yolks, at room temperature
1 teaspoon white wine vinegar
½ pint/300 ml oil, at room temperature
salt and white pepper
1 teaspoon lemon juice

Rinse a wide, shallow bowl with hot water and dry it well.
1. Put the egg yolks in the bowl, add 2-3 drops of vinegar and mix with a wire whisk.
2. Add the oil, drop by drop, constantly whisking.
3. When the mixture becomes thick and creamy add the oil in a thin, slow stream, still whisking, until it turns paler in colour.
If the mayonnaise becomes too thick before all the oil is used, stir in a few drops of lemon juice and continue whisking in the remaining oil.
Season with salt and pepper and sharpen with a little lemon juice.

1.

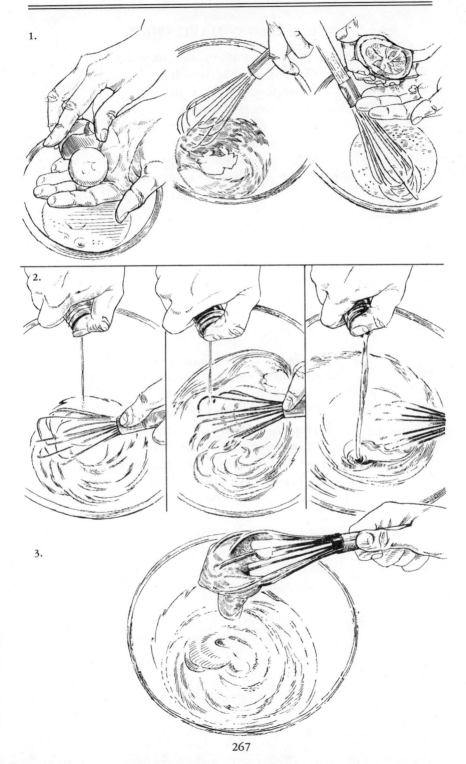

2.

3.

QUICK LEMON MAYONNAISE

2 large egg yolks, at room temperature
5 teaspoons lemon juice
1 teaspoon Dijon mustard
pinch of sugar
pinch of cayenne pepper
¼ teaspoon salt
¼ teaspoon white pepper
½ pint/300 ml olive or vegetable oil
a little single cream to thin the mayonnaise if desired

In an electric blender or mixer combine the egg yolks, lemon juice, mustard, sugar, cayenne, salt and pepper.
Blend at high speed for 30 seconds, then add the oil in a thin slow stream until the mixture thickens.

GREEN MAYONNAISE

2 tablespoons fresh parsley, chopped
1 tablespoon fresh chives, chopped
1 tablespoon fresh tarragon, chopped, OR
1 teaspoon dried tarragon
1 tablespoon fresh dill, chopped, OR
1 teaspoon dried dill weed
1 teaspoon fresh chervil, chopped, OR
¼ teaspoon dried chervil
8 oz/225 g mayonnaise, see page 266

Fold all the herbs into the mayonnaise.
Let the mayonnaise stand at room temperature for 25-30 minutes.

GARLIC MAYONNAISE

4 cloves of garlic
salt
2 egg yolks, at room temperature
½ pint/300 ml olive or vegetable oil
white pepper
2 tablespoons white wine vinegar

Peel and crush the garlic in a large mortar with a little salt.
Drop in the egg yolks, one at a time, mixing them into the
garlic with a wire whisk.
Add the oil, drop by drop, and when the mixture thickens,
add it in a slow stream.
Whisk in the vinegar to sharpen the taste, add white pepper
and more salt if required.

QUICK CURRY MAYONNAISE

1 egg yolk, at room temperature
5 teaspoons lemon juice
1½ teaspoons curry powder
1 teaspoon Dijon mustard
1 small clove of garlic, crushed
¼ teaspoon salt
¼ teaspoon white pepper
½ pint/300 ml olive or vegetable oil

In an electric blender or mixer combine the egg yolk, lemon
juice, curry powder, mustard, garlic, salt and pepper.
Blend at high speed, then add the oil in a slow stream until
the mixture thickens.

BÉCHAMEL SAUCE

2 oz/50 g butter
1½ oz/40 g flour
¼ pint/425 ml milk
salt and white pepper

Melt the butter in a saucepan over medium heat.
Work in the flour with a wooden spoon. When the mixture froths take the pan off the heat and add the milk in a slow stream, stirring constantly. When the sauce is smooth return the pan to the heat and bring to simmering point.
Season with salt and pepper to taste and continue cooking for 10 minutes. Stir frequently.
If the sauce is too thick, add a little more milk.

QUICK BÉCHAMEL SAUCE

2 oz/50 g butter
1½ oz/40 g flour
¾ pint/425 ml hot milk
pinch of grated nutmeg
1 bay leaf
salt and white pepper

Melt the butter in a saucepan and add the flour, stirring, until it is well blended. Add the hot mik, little by little, stirring continually, until the sauce begins to thicken.
Add the nutmeg, bay leaf, salt and pepper to taste.
Reduce the heat and cook slowly, stirring frequently, for 5 minutes. Discard the bay leaf.

HOLLANDAISE SAUCE

8 oz/225 g unsalted butter, softened
4 egg yolks, at room temperature
1 tablespoon cold water
juice of 1 lemon
salt and white pepper

The secret of this sauce is that it must never boil.

Divide the butter into 4 equal pieces and set aside.

Combine the lemon juice, water, salt and pepper in the top of a double saucepan or in a *bain-marie*.

Add the egg yolks and whisk in the butter, one piece at a time, making sure that each piece is melted before adding the next.

Stir the mixture vigorously all the time with a wire whisk over hot, but not boiling, water.

Whisk until the sauce thickens, then add lemon juice and salt and pepper to taste.

The water in the *bain-marie* must remain at a constant temperature. The sauce can be kept warm, covered with greaseproof paper, over a pan of warm water.

TOMATO SAUCE

1 clove of garlic, crushed
1 shallot, finely chopped
1 medium onion, finely chopped
3 tablespoons olive oil
2¼ lb/1 kg ripe tomatoes
sprig of thyme, OR
¼ teaspoon dried thyme
1 bay leaf
1 lump of sugar
salt and freshly ground black pepper

In a large saucepan gently cook the garlic, shallot, and onion in the olive oil until soft but not browned.

Chop the tomatoes and add them to the onion mixture. Add the thyme, bay leaf and sugar.

Stir and season with salt and plenty of freshly ground black pepper.

Cover the pan and simmer for 1 hour; then simmer uncovered until the sauce has thickened to a purée.

Remove the bay leaf and the thyme, and with a wooden spoon work the purée through a sieve.

Correct the seasoning.

TARTAR SAUCE
Sauce Tartare

4 gherkins, finely chopped
3 shallots, finely chopped
1 egg yolk, hard-boiled and finely chopped
1 tablespoon capers, chopped
1 tablespoon fresh parsley, finely chopped
1 tablespoon onion, grated
1 tablespoon fresh tarragon, chopped, OR
1 teaspoon dried tarragon
1 tablespoon fresh chervil, chopped, OR
1 teaspoon dried chervil
1 teaspoon Dijon mustard
1 teaspoon fresh lemon juice
1 teaspoon sugar
freshly ground white pepper
12 fl oz/350 ml mayonnaise, see page 266

Into the mayonnaise fold the gherkins, shallots, egg yolk, capers, parsley, onion, tarragon, chervil, mustard, lemon juice, sugar, white pepper and salt to taste.